Praise for *Think Like a Freak*

"Utterly captivating. . . . Makes the world a better place. It is also a lot of fun."

—Malcolm Gladwell, *New York Times*
bestselling author of *Blink*,
The Tipping Point, and *David and Goliath*

"Over nine entertaining chapters [Levitt and Dubner] demonstrate how not to fall into hackneyed approaches to solving problems and concretely illustrate how to reframe questions."

—*Daily News* (New York)

"Compelling and fun."

—*New York Post*

"This book will change your life."   —*Daily Express* (London)

"Good ideas . . . expressed with panache."

—*Financial Times* (London)

"An interesting and thought-provoking read."   —The Horn

"Full of ideas. . . . Wears its cleverness lightly."

—*Daily Mail* (London)

Also by Steven D. Levitt & Stephen J. Dubner

FREAKONOMICS

A Rogue Economist Explores
the Hidden Side of Everything

SUPERFREAKONOMICS

Global Cooling, Patriotic Prostitutes, and
Why Suicide Bombers Should Buy Life Insurance

SUPERFREAKONOMICS

The Super-Deluxe, Super-Illustrated Edition

Also by Stephen J. Dubner

TURBULENT SOULS

A Catholic Son's Return to His Jewish Family

• *also published as* •

Choosing My Religion: A Memoir of a
Family Beyond Belief

CONFESSIONS OF A HERO-WORSHIPER

THE BOY WITH TWO BELLY BUTTONS

THINK
LIKE A
FREAK

THE AUTHORS OF *FREAKONOMICS* OFFER
TO RETRAIN YOUR BRAIN

STEVEN D. LEVITT &
STEPHEN J. DUBNER

WM

William Morrow
An Imprint of HarperCollinsPublishers

HarperCollins books may be purchased for educational, business, or sales promotional use. For information please e-mail the Special Markets Department at SPsales@harpercollins.com.

A hardcover edition of this book was published in 2014 by William Morrow, an imprint of HarperCollins Publishers.

FIRST WILLIAM MORROW PAPERBACK EDITION PUBLISHED 2015.

Library of Congress Cataloging-in-Publication Data has been applied for.

ISBN 978-0-06-221834-6

16 17 18 19 OV/RRD 10 9 8 7 6

For ELLEN,
who has been there for everything,
including the books.

—SJD

For my sister LINDA LEVITT JINES,
whose creative genius amazed,
amused, and inspired me.

—SDL

Contents

CONTENTS

What does Martin Luther have to do with the German economy? . . . How the "Scramble for Africa" created lasting strife . . . Why did slave traders lick the skin of the slaves they bought? . . . Medicine vs. folklore . . . Consider the ulcer . . . The first blockbuster drugs . . . Why did the young doctor swallow a batch of dangerous bacteria? . . . Talk about gastric upset! . . . The universe that lives in our gut . . . The power of poop.

How to have good ideas . . . The power of thinking small . . . Smarter kids at $15 a pop . . . Don't be afraid of the obvious . . . 1.6 million of anything is a lot . . . Don't be seduced by complexity . . . What to look for in a junkyard . . . The human body is just a machine . . . Freaks just want to have fun . . . It is hard to get good at something you don't like . . . Is a "no-lose lottery" the answer to our low savings rate? . . . Gambling meets charity . . . Why kids figure out magic tricks better than adults . . . "You'd think scientists would be hard to dupe" . . . How to smuggle childlike instincts across the adult border.

It's the incentives, stupid! . . . A girl, a bag of candy, and a toilet . . . What financial incentives can and can't do . . . The giant milk necklace . . . Cash for grades . . . With financial incentives, size matters . . . How to determine someone's true incentives . . . Riding the herd mentality . . . Why are moral incentives so weak? . . . Let's steal some petrified wood! . . . One of the most rad-

car save? . . . Keep the insults to yourself . . . Why you should tell stories . . . Is eating fat really so bad? . . . The Encyclopedia of Ethical Failure . . . *What is the Bible "about"? . . . The Ten Commandments versus* The Brady Bunch.

Winston Churchill was right—and wrong . . . The sunk-cost fallacy and opportunity cost . . . You can't solve tomorrow's problem if you won't abandon today's dud . . . Celebrating failure with a party and cake . . . Why the flagship Chinese store did not open on time . . . Were the Challenger's *O-rings bound to fail? . . . Learn how you might fail without going to the trouble of failing . . . The $1 million question: "when to struggle and when to quit" . . . Would you let a coin toss decide your future? . . . "Should I quit the Mormon faith?" . . . Growing a beard will not make you happy . . . But ditching your girlfriend might . . . Why Dubner and Levitt are so fond of quitting . . . This whole book was about "letting go" . . . And now it's your turn.*

THINK
LIKE A
FREAK

CHAPTER 1

What Does It Mean to Think Like a Freak?

After writing *Freakonomics* and *SuperFreakonomics,* we started to hear from readers with all sorts of questions. *Is a college degree still "worth it"?* (Short answer: yes; long answer: also yes.) *Is it a good idea to pass along a family business to the next generation?* (Sure, if your goal is to kill off the business—for the data show it's generally better to bring in an outside manager.*) *Whatever happened to the carpal tunnel syndrome epidemic?* (Once journalists stopped getting it, they stopped writing about it—but the problem persists, especially among blue-collar workers.)

Some questions were existential: *What makes people truly happy? Is income inequality as dangerous as it seems? Would a diet high in omega-3 lead to world peace?*

---

* Family firms in Japan have a long-standing solution to this problem: they find a new CEO from outside the family and legally adopt him. That is why nearly 100 percent of adoptees in Japan are adult males.

People wanted to know the pros and cons of: autonomous vehicles, breast-feeding, chemotherapy, estate taxes, fracking, lotteries, "medicinal prayer," online dating, patent reform, rhino poaching, using an iron off the tee, and virtual currencies. One minute we'd get an e-mail asking us to "solve the obesity epidemic" and then, five minutes later, one urging us to "wipe out famine, right now!"

Readers seemed to think no riddle was too tricky, no problem too hard, that it couldn't be sorted out. It was as if we owned some proprietary tool—a Freakonomics forceps, one might imagine—that could be plunged into the body politic to extract some buried wisdom.

If only that were true!

The fact is that solving problems is hard. If a given problem still exists, you can bet that a lot of people have already come along and failed to solve it. Easy problems evaporate; it is the hard ones that linger. Furthermore, it takes a lot of time to track down, organize, and analyze the data to answer even one small question well.*

So rather than trying and probably failing to answer most of the questions sent our way, we wondered if it might be better to write a book that can teach anyone to think like a Freak.

What might that look like?

---

* See Notes on page 215 for all underlying research citations and other background information.

• • •

Imagine you are a soccer player, a very fine one, and you've led your nation to the brink of a World Cup championship. All you must do now is make a single penalty kick. The odds are in your favor: roughly 75 percent of penalty kicks at the elite level are successful.

The crowd bellows as you place the ball on the chalked penalty mark. The goal is a mere 12 yards away; it is 8 yards across and 8 feet high.

The goalkeeper stares you down. Once the ball rockets off your boot, it will travel toward him at 80 miles per hour. At such a speed, he can ill afford to wait and see where you kick the ball; he must take a guess and fling his body in that direction. If the keeper guesses wrong, your odds rise to about 90 percent.

The best shot is a kick toward a corner of the goal with enough force that the keeper cannot make the save even if he guesses correctly. But such a shot leaves little margin for error: a slight miskick, and you'll miss the goal completely. So you may want to ease up a bit, or aim slightly away from the corner—although that gives the keeper a better chance if he does guess correctly.

You must also choose between the left corner and the right. If you are a right-footed kicker, as most players are, going left is your "strong" side. That translates to more power and accuracy—but of course the keeper knows this too. That's why keepers jump toward the kicker's left corner 57 percent of the time, and to the right only 41.

So there you stand—the crowd in full throat, your heart in hyperspeed—preparing to take this life-changing kick. The eyes of the world are upon you, and the prayers of your nation. If the ball goes in, your name will forever be spoken in the tone reserved for the most beloved saints. If you fail— well, better not to think about that.

The options swirl through your head. Strong side or weak? Do you go hard for the corner or play it a bit safe? Have you taken penalty kicks against this keeper before— and if so, where did you aim? And where did he jump? As you think all this through, you also think about what the keeper is thinking, and you may even think about what the keeper is thinking about what you are thinking.

You know the chance of becoming a hero is about 75 percent, which isn't bad. But wouldn't it be nice to jack up that number? Might there be a better way to think about this problem? What if you could outfox your opponent by thinking beyond the obvious? You know the keeper is optimizing between jumping right and left. But what if . . . what if . . . what if you kick neither right nor left? What if you do the silliest thing imaginable and kick into the dead center of the goal?

Yes, that is where the keeper is standing now, but you are pretty sure he will vacate that spot as you begin your kick. Remember what the data say: keepers jump left 57 percent of the time and right 41 percent—which means they stay in

WHAT DOES IT MEAN TO THINK LIKE A FREAK?

the center only 2 times out of 100. A leaping keeper may of course still stop a ball aimed at the center, but how often can that happen? If only you could see the data on all penalty kicks taken toward the center of the goal!

Okay, we just happen to have that: a kick toward the center, as risky as it may appear, is seven percentage points *more* likely to succeed than a kick to the corner.

Are you willing to take the chance?

Let's say you are. You trot toward the ball, plant your left foot, load up the right, and let it fly. You are instantaneously gripped by a bone-shaking roar—*Goooooooooal!* The crowd erupts in an orgasmic rush as you are buried beneath a mountain of teammates. This moment will last forever; the rest of your life will be one big happy party; your children grow up to be strong, prosperous, and kind. Congratulations!

While a penalty kick aimed at the center of the goal is significantly more likely to succeed, only 17 percent of kicks are aimed there. Why so few?

One reason is that at first glance, aiming center looks like a terrible idea. Kicking the ball straight at the goalkeeper? That just seems unnatural, an obvious violation of common sense—but then so did the idea of preventing a disease by injecting people with the very microbes that cause it.

Furthermore, one advantage the kicker has on a penalty

kick is mystery: the keeper doesn't know where he will aim. If kickers did the same thing every time, their success rate would plummet; if they started going center more often, keepers would adapt.

There is a third and important reason why more kickers don't aim center, especially in a high-stakes setting like the World Cup. But no soccer player in his right mind would ever admit it: the fear of shame.

Imagine again you are the player about to take that penalty kick. At this most turbulent moment, what is your true incentive? The answer might seem obvious: you want to score the goal to win the game for your team. If that's the case, the statistics plainly show you should kick the ball dead center. But is winning the game your truest incentive?

Picture yourself standing over the ball. You have just mentally committed to aiming for the center. But wait a minute—what if the goalkeeper *doesn't* dive? What if for some reason he stays at home and you kick the ball straight into his gut, and he saves *his* country without even having to budge? How pathetic you will seem! Now the keeper is the hero and you must move your family abroad to avoid assassination.

So you reconsider.

You think about going the traditional route, toward a corner. If the keeper does guess correctly and stops the ball—well, you will have made a valiant effort even if it was bested by a more valiant one. No, you won't become a hero, but nor will you have to flee the country.

If you follow this selfish incentive—protecting your own reputation by not doing something potentially foolish—you are more likely to kick toward a corner.

If you follow the communal incentive—trying to win the game for your nation even though you risk looking personally foolish—you will kick toward the center.

Sometimes in life, going straight up the middle is the boldest move of all.

If asked how we'd behave in a situation that pits a private benefit against the greater good, most of us won't admit to favoring the private benefit. But as history clearly shows, most people, whether because of nature or nurture, generally put their own interests ahead of others'. This doesn't make them bad people; it just makes them human.

But all this self-interest can be frustrating if your ambitions are larger than simply securing some small private victory. Maybe you want to ease poverty, or make government work better, or persuade your company to pollute less, or just get your kids to stop fighting. How are you supposed to get everyone to pull in the same direction when they are all pulling primarily for themselves?

We wrote this book to answer that sort of question. It strikes us that in recent years, the idea has arisen that there is a "right" way to think about solving a given problem and of course a "wrong" way too. This inevitably leads to a lot of shouting—and, sadly, a lot of unsolved problems. Can this situation be improved upon? We hope so. We'd like to bury the idea that there's a right way and a wrong way, a smart way and a foolish way, a red way and a blue way. The modern world demands that we all think a bit more productively, more creatively, more rationally; that we think from a different angle, with a different set of muscles, with a different set of expectations; that we think with neither fear nor favor, with neither blind optimism nor sour skepticism. That we think like—ahem—a Freak.

Our first two books were animated by a relatively simple set of ideas:

Incentives are the cornerstone of modern life. And understanding them—or, often, deciphering them—is the key to understanding a problem, and how it might be solved.

Knowing what to measure, and how to measure it, can make a complicated world less so. There is nothing like the sheer power of numbers to scrub away layers of confusion and contradiction, especially with emotional, hot-button topics.

The conventional wisdom is often wrong. And a blithe acceptance of it can lead to sloppy, wasteful, or even dangerous outcomes.

Correlation does not equal causality. When two things travel together, it is tempting to assume that one causes the other. Married people, for instance, are demonstrably happier than single people; does this mean that marriage causes happiness? Not necessarily. The data suggest that happy people are more likely to get married in the first place. As one researcher memorably put it, "If you're grumpy, who the hell wants to marry you?"

This book builds on these same core ideas, but there is a difference. The first two books were rarely prescriptive. For the most part, we simply used data to tell stories we found interesting, shining a light on parts of society that often lay in shadow. This book steps out of the shadows and tries to offer some advice that may occasionally be useful, whether you are interested in minor lifehacks or major global reforms.

That said, this isn't a self-help book in the traditional sense. We are probably not the kind of people you'd typically want to ask for help; and some of our advice tends to get people into trouble rather than out of it.

Our thinking is inspired by what is known as the economic approach. That doesn't mean focusing on "the economy"—far from it. The economic approach is both broader and simpler than that. It relies on data, rather than hunch or ideology, to understand how the world works, to learn how incentives succeed (or fail), how resources get allocated, and what sort of obstacles prevent people from getting those resources, whether they are concrete (like food and transportation) or more aspirational (like education and love).

There is nothing magical about this way of thinking. It usually traffics in the obvious and places a huge premium on common sense. So here's the bad news: if you come to this book hoping for the equivalent of a magician spilling his secrets, you may be disappointed. But there's good news too: thinking like a Freak is simple enough that anyone can do it. What's perplexing is that so few people do.

Why is that?

One reason is that it's easy to let your biases—political, intellectual, or otherwise—color your view of the world. A growing body of research suggests that even the smartest people tend to seek out evidence that confirms what they already think, rather than new information that would give them a more robust view of reality.

It's also tempting to run with a herd. Even on the most important issues of the day, we often adopt the views of our friends, families, and colleagues. (You'll read more on this in Chapter 6.) On some level, this makes sense: it is easier to fall in line with what your family and friends think than to find new family and friends! But running with the herd means we are quick to embrace the status quo, slow to change our minds, and happy to delegate our thinking.

Another barrier to thinking like a Freak is that most people are too busy to rethink the way they think—or to even spend much time thinking at all. When was the last time you sat for an hour of pure, unadulterated thinking? If you're like most people, it's been a while. Is this simply a function of our high-speed era? Perhaps not. The absurdly talented George Bernard Shaw—a world-class writer *and* a founder of the London School of Economics—noted this thought deficit many years ago. "Few people think more than two or three times a year," Shaw reportedly said. "I have made an international reputation for myself by thinking once or twice a week."

We too try to think once or twice a week (though surely not as cleverly as Shaw) and encourage you to do the same.

This is not to say you should necessarily *want* to think like a Freak. It presents some potential downsides. You may find yourself way, way out of step with the prevailing winds. You might occasionally say things that make other people squirm. Perhaps, for instance, you meet a lovely, conscientious couple with three children, and find yourself blurting out that child car seats are a waste of time and money (at least that's what the crash-test data say). Or, at a holiday dinner with your new girlfriend's family, you blather on about how the local-food movement can actually hurt the environment—only to learn that her father is a hard-core locavore, and everything on the table was grown within fifty miles.

You'll have to grow accustomed to people calling you a crank, or sputtering with indignation, or perhaps even getting up and walking out of the room. We have some first-hand experience with this.

Shortly after the publication of *SuperFreakonomics,* while on book tour in England, we were invited to meet with David Cameron, who would soon become prime minister of the United Kingdom.

While it is not uncommon for people like him to solicit ideas from people like us, the invitation surprised us. In the opening pages of *SuperFreakonomics,* we declared that we knew next to nothing about the macroeconomic forces— inflation, unemployment, and the like—that politicians seek to control by yanking a lever this way or that.

What's more, politicians tend to shy away from controversy, and our book had already generated its fair share in the U.K. We had been grilled on national TV about a chapter that described an algorithm we created, in concert with a British bank, to identify suspected terrorists. Why on earth, the TV interviewers asked us, did we disclose the secrets that might help terrorists avoid detection? (We couldn't answer that question at the time, but we do in Chapter 7 of this book. Hint: the disclosure was not an accident.)

We had also taken heat for suggesting that the standard playbook for fighting global warming was not going to work. In fact, the Cameron operative who collected us at the security post, a sharp young policy adviser named Rohan Silva, told us that his neighborhood bookshop refused to carry *SuperFreakonomics* because the shop's owner so hated our global-warming chapter.

Silva took us to a conference room where roughly two dozen Cameron advisers waited. Their boss hadn't yet arrived. Most of them were in their twenties or thirties. One gentleman, a once and future cabinet minister, was significantly more senior. He took the floor and told us that, upon election, the Cameron administration would fight global warming tooth and nail. If it were up to him, he said, Britain would become a zero-carbon society overnight. It was, he said, "a matter of the highest moral obligation."

This made our ears prick up. One thing we've learned is that when people, especially politicians, start making decisions based on a reading of their moral compass, facts tend to be among the first casualties. We asked the minister what he meant by "moral obligation."

"If it weren't for England," he continued, "the world wouldn't be in the state it's in. None of *this* would have happened." He gestured upward and outward. The "this," he implied, meant this room, this building, the city of London, all of civilization.

We must have looked puzzled, for he explained further. England, he said, having started the Industrial Revolution, led the rest of the world down the path toward pollution, environmental degradation, and global warming. It was therefore England's obligation to take the lead in undoing the damage.

Just then Mr. Cameron burst through the door. "All right," he boomed, "where are the clever people?"

He wore crisp white shirtsleeves, his trademark purple tie, and an air of irrepressible optimism. As we chatted, it became instantly clear why he was projected to become the next prime minister. Everything about him radiated competence and confidence. He looked to be exactly the sort of man whom deans at Eton and Oxford envision when they are first handed the boy.

Cameron said the biggest problem he would inherit as prime minister was a gravely ill economy. The U.K., along with the rest of the world, was still in the grip of a crushing recession. The mood, from pensioners to students to industry titans, was morose; the national debt was enormous and climbing. Immediately upon taking office, Cameron told us, he would need to make broad and deep cuts.

But, he added, there were a few precious, inalienable rights that he would protect at any cost.

Like what? we asked.

"Well, the National Health Service," he said, eyes alight with pride. This made sense. The NHS provides cradle-to-grave health care for every Briton, most of it free at point of use. The oldest and largest such system in the world, it is as much a part of the national fabric as association football and spotted dick. One former chancellor of the exchequer called the NHS "the closest thing the English have to a religion"—which is doubly interesting since England does have an actual religion.

There was just one problem: U.K. health-care costs had more than doubled over the previous ten years and were expected to keep rising.

Although we didn't know it at the time, Cameron's devotion to the NHS was based in part on an intense personal experience. His eldest child, Ivan, was born with a rare neurological disorder called Ohtahara syndrome. It is marked by frequent, violent seizures. As a result, the Cameron family had become all too familiar with NHS nurses, doctors, ambulances, and hospitals. "When your family relies on the NHS all the time, day after day, night after night, you really know just how precious it is," he once told the Conservative Party's annual conference. Ivan died in early 2009, a few months short of his seventh birthday.

So perhaps it was no surprise that Cameron, even as head of a party that embraced fiscal austerity, should view the NHS as sacrosanct. To monkey with the system, even during an economic crisis, would make as much political sense as drop-kicking one of the Queen's corgis.

But that didn't mean it made *practical* sense. While the goal of free, unlimited, lifetime health care is laudable, the economics are tricky. We now pointed this out, as respectfully as possible, to the presumptive prime minister.

Because there is so much emotion attached to health care, it can be hard to see that it is, by and large, like any other part of the economy. But under a setup like the U.K.'s, health care is virtually the only part of the economy where individuals can go out and get nearly any service they need and pay close to zero, whether the actual cost of the procedure is $100 or $100,000.

What's wrong with that? When people don't pay the true cost of something, they tend to consume it inefficiently.

Think of the last time you sat down at an all-you-can-eat restaurant. How likely were you to eat a bit more than normal? The same thing happens if health care is distributed in a similar fashion: people consume more of it than if they were charged the sticker price. This means the "worried well" crowd out the truly sick, wait times increase for everyone, and a massive share of the costs go to the final months of elderly patients' lives, often without much real advantage.

This sort of overconsumption can be more easily tolerated when health care is only a small part of the economy. But with health-care costs approaching 10 percent of GDP in the U.K.—and nearly *double* that in the United States—you have to seriously rethink how it is provided, and paid for.

We tried to make our point with a thought experiment. We suggested to Mr. Cameron that he consider a similar policy in a different arena. What if, for instance, every Briton were also entitled to a free, unlimited, lifetime supply of transportation? That is, what if everyone were allowed to go down to the car dealership whenever they wanted and pick out any new model, free of charge, and drive it home?

We expected him to light up and say, "Well, yes, that'd be patently absurd—there'd be no reason to maintain your old car, and everyone's incentives would be skewed. I see your point about all this free health care we're doling out!"

But he said no such thing. In fact he didn't say anything at all. The smile did not leave David Cameron's face, but it did leave his eyes. Maybe our story hadn't come out as we'd intended. Or maybe it did, and that was the problem. In any case, he offered a quick handshake and hurried off to find a less-ridiculous set of people with whom to meet.

You could hardly blame him. Fixing a huge problem like runaway health-care costs is about a thousand times harder than, say, figuring out how to take a penalty kick. (That's why, as we argue in Chapter 5, you should focus on small problems whenever possible.) We also could have profited from knowing then what we know now about persuading people who don't want to be persuaded (which we cover in Chapter 8).

That said, we fervently believe there is a huge upside in retraining your brain to think differently about problems large and small. In this book, we share everything we've learned over the past several years, some of which has worked out better than our brief encounter with the prime minister.

Are you willing to give it a try? Excellent! The first step is to not be embarrassed by how much you don't yet know. . . .

CHAPTER 2

The Three Hardest Words in the English Language

Imagine you are asked to listen to a simple story and then answer a few questions about it. Here's the story:

> *A little girl named Mary goes to the beach with her mother and brother. They drive there in a red car. At the beach they swim, eat some ice cream, play in the sand, and have sandwiches for lunch.*

Now the questions:

1. What color was the car?
2. Did they have fish and chips for lunch?
3. Did they listen to music in the car?
4. Did they drink lemonade with lunch?

All right, how'd you do? Let's compare your answers to those of a bunch of British schoolchildren, aged five to nine, who were given this quiz by academic researchers. Nearly all the children got the first two questions right ("red" and "no"). But the children did much worse with questions 3 and 4. Why? Those questions were unanswerable—there simply wasn't enough information given in the story. And yet a whopping 76 percent of the children answered these questions either yes or no.

Kids who try to bluff their way through a simple quiz like this are right on track for careers in business and politics, where almost no one ever admits to not knowing anything. It has long been said that the three hardest words to say in the English language are *I love you*. We heartily disagree! For most people, it is much harder to say *I don't know*. That's a shame, for until you can admit what you don't yet know, it's virtually impossible to learn what you need to.

Before we get into the reasons for all this fakery—and the costs, and the solutions—let's clarify what we mean when we talk about what we "know."

There are of course different levels and categories of knowledge. At the top of this hierarchy are what might be called "known facts," things that can be scientifically verified. (As Daniel Patrick Moynihan was famous for saying: "Everyone's entitled to their own opinion but not to their own facts.") If you insist that the chemical composition of water is HO_2 instead of H_2O, you will eventually be proved wrong.

Then there are "beliefs," things we hold to be true but which may not be easily verified. On such topics, there is more room for disagreement. For instance: Does the devil really exist?

This question was asked in a global survey. Among the countries included, here are the top five for devil belief, ranked by share of believers:

1. Malta (84.5%)
2. Northern Ireland (75.6%)
3. United States (69.1%)
4. Ireland (55.3%)
5. Canada (42.9%)

And here are the five countries with the fewest devil believers:

1. Latvia (9.1%)
2. Bulgaria (9.6%)
3. Denmark (10.4%)
4. Sweden (12.0%)
5. Czech Republic (12.8%)

How can there be such a deep split on such a simple question? Either the Latvians or the Maltese plainly don't know what they think they know.

Okay, so maybe the devil's existence is too otherworldly a topic to consider at all factual. Let's look at a different kind of question, one that falls somewhere between belief and fact:

> *According to news reports, groups of Arabs carried out the attacks against the USA on September 11. Do you believe this to be true or not?*

To most of us, the very question is absurd: *of course* it is true! But when asked in predominantly Muslim countries, the question got a different answer. Only 20 percent of Indonesians believed that Arabs carried out the 9/11 attacks, along with 11 percent of Kuwaitis and 4 percent of Pakistanis. (When asked who *was* responsible, respondents typically blamed the Israeli or U.S. government or "non-Muslim terrorists.")

All right, so what we "know" can plainly be sculpted by political or religious views. The world is also thick with "entrepreneurs of error," as the economist Edward Glaeser calls them, political and religious and business leaders who "supply beliefs when it will increase their own financial or political returns."

On its own, this is problem enough. But the stakes get higher when we routinely pretend to know more than we do.

Think about some of the hard issues that politicians and business leaders face every day. *What's the best way to stop mass shootings? Are the benefits of fracking worth the environmental costs? What happens if we allow that Middle Eastern dictator who hates us to stay in power?*

Questions like these can't be answered merely by assembling a cluster of facts; they require judgment, intuition, and a guess as to how things will ultimately play out. Furthermore, these are multidimensional cause-and-effect questions, which means their outcomes are both distant and nuanced. With complex issues, it can be ridiculously hard to pin a particular cause on a given effect. *Did the assault-weapon ban really cut crime—or was it one of ten other factors? Did the economy stall because tax rates were too high—or were the real villains all those Chinese exports and a spike in oil prices?*

In other words, it can be hard to *ever* really "know" what caused or solved a given problem—and that's for events that have already happened. Just think how much harder it is to predict what will work in the future. "Prediction," as Niels Bohr liked to say, "is very difficult, especially if it's about the future."

And yet we constantly hear from experts—not just politicians and business leaders but also sports pundits, stock-market gurus, and of course meteorologists—who tell us they have a pretty good idea of how the future will unspool. Do they really know what they're talking about or are they, like the British schoolkids, just bluffing?

In recent years, scholars have begun to systematically track the predictions of various experts. One of the most impressive studies was conducted by Philip Tetlock, a psychology professor at the University of Pennsylvania. His focus is politics. Tetlock enlisted nearly 300 experts—

government officials, political-science scholars, national-security experts, and economists—to make thousands of predictions that he charted over the course of twenty years. For instance: in Democracy X—let's say it's Brazil—will the current majority party retain, lose, or strengthen its status after the next election? Or, for Undemocratic Country Y—Syria, perhaps—will the basic character of the political regime change in the next five years? In the next ten years? If so, in what direction?

The results of Tetlock's study were sobering. These most expert of experts—96 percent of them had postgraduate training—"thought they knew more than they knew," he says. How accurate were their predictions? They weren't much better than "dart-throwing chimps," as Tetlock often joked.

"Oh, the monkey-with-a-dartboard comparison, that comes back to haunt me all the time," he says. "But with respect to how they did relative to, say, a baseline group of Berkeley undergraduates making predictions, they did somewhat better than that. Did they do better than an extrapolation algorithm? No, they did not."

Tetlock's "extrapolation algorithm" is simply a computer programmed to predict "no change in current situation." Which, if you think about it, is a computer's way of saying "I don't know."

A similar study by a firm called CXO Advisory Group covered more than 6,000 predictions by stock-market experts over several years. It found an overall accuracy rate of 47.4 percent. Again, the dart-throwing chimp likely would have done just as well—and, when you consider investment fees, at a fraction of the cost.

When asked to name the attributes of someone who is particularly bad at predicting, Tetlock needed just one word. "Dogmatism," he says. That is, an unshakable belief they know something to be true even when they don't. Tetlock and other scholars who have tracked prominent pundits find that they tend to be "massively overconfident," in Tetlock's words, even when their predictions prove stone-cold wrong. That is a lethal combination—cocky plus wrong—especially when a more prudent option exists: simply admit that the future is far less knowable than you think.

Unfortunately, this rarely happens. Smart people love to make smart-sounding predictions, no matter how wrong they may turn out to be. This phenomenon was beautifully captured in a 1998 article for *Red Herring* magazine called "Why Most Economists' Predictions Are Wrong." It was written by Paul Krugman, himself an economist, who went on to win the Nobel Prize.* Krugman points out that too many economists' predictions fail because they overesti-

---

* The Nobel economics award, instituted in 1969, is not one of the original and therefore official Nobel Prizes, which since 1906 have been issued in Physics, Chemistry, Physiology or Medicine, Literature, and Peace. Instead, the economics award is officially called the Sveriges Riksbank Prize in Economic Sciences in Memory of Alfred Nobel. There are continuing arguments as to whether the economics award should in fact be called a "Nobel Prize." While we sympathize with the historians and semanticists who argue against it, we see no harm in conforming to what has become the accepted usage.

mate the impact of future technologies, and then he makes a few predictions of his own. Here's one: "The growth of the Internet will slow drastically, as the flaw in 'Metcalfe's law'—which states that the number of potential connections in a network is proportional to the square of the number of participants—becomes apparent: most people have nothing to say to each other! By 2005 or so, it will become clear that the Internet's impact on the economy has been no greater than the fax machine's."

As of this writing, the market capitalization of Google, Amazon, and Facebook alone is more than $700 billion, which is more than the GDP of all but eighteen countries. If you throw in Apple, which isn't an Internet company but couldn't exist without it, the market cap is $1.2 *trillion*. That could buy a lot of fax machines.

Maybe we need more economists like Thomas Sargent. He too won a Nobel, for his work measuring macroeconomic cause and effect. Sargent has likely forgotten more about inflation and interest rates than the rest of us will ever know. When Ally Bank wanted to make a TV commercial a few years ago touting a certificate of deposit with a "raise your rate" feature, Sargent was cast in the lead.

The setting is an auditorium whose stage evokes a university club: ornate chandeliers, orderly bookshelves, walls hung with portraits of distinguished gentlemen. Sargent, seated regally in a leather club chair, awaits his introduction. A moderator begins:

MODERATOR: Tonight, our guest: Thomas Sargent, Nobel laureate in economics and one of the most-cited economists in the world. Professor Sargent, can you tell me what CD rates will be in two years?

SARGENT: No.

And that's it. As the Ally announcer points out, "If he can't, no one can"—thus the need for an adjustable-rate CD. The ad is a work of comic genius. Why? Because Sargent, in giving the only correct answer to a virtually unanswerable question, shows how absurd it is that so many of us routinely fail to do the same.

It isn't only that we know less than we pretend about the outside world; we don't even know ourselves all that well. Most people are terrible at the seemingly simple task of assessing their own talents. As two psychologists recently put it in an academic journal: "Despite spending more time with themselves than with any other person, people often have surprisingly poor insight into their skills and abilities." A classic example: when asked to rate their driving skills, roughly 80 percent of respondents rated themselves better than the average driver.

But let's say you *are* excellent at a given thing, a true master of your domain, like Thomas Sargent. Does this mean you are also more likely to excel in a different domain?

A sizable body of research says the answer is no. The

takeaway here is simple but powerful: just because you're great at something doesn't mean you're good at everything. Unfortunately, this fact is routinely ignored by those who engage in—take a deep breath—*ultracrepidarianism,* or "the habit of giving opinions and advice on matters outside of one's knowledge or competence."

Making grandiose assumptions about your abilities and failing to acknowledge what you don't know can lead, unsurprisingly, to disaster. When schoolchildren fake their answers about a trip to the seashore, there are no consequences; their reluctance to say "I don't know" imposes no real costs on anyone. But in the real world, the societal costs of faking it can be huge.

Consider the Iraq War. It was executed primarily on U.S. claims that Saddam Hussein had weapons of mass destruction and was in league with al Qaeda. To be sure, there was more to it than that—politics, oil, and perhaps revenge—but it was the al Qaeda and weapons claims that sealed the deal. Eight years, $800 billion, and nearly 4,500 American deaths later—along with at least 100,000 Iraqi fatalities—it was tempting to consider what might have happened had the purveyors of those claims admitted that they did not in fact "know" them to be true.

Just as a warm and moist environment is conducive to the spread of deadly bacteria, the worlds of politics and business especially—with their long time frames, complex outcomes, and murky cause and effect—are conducive to the spread of half-cocked guesses posing as fact. And here's why: the people making these wild guesses can usually get away with it! By the time things have played out and everyone has realized they didn't know what they were talking about, the bluffers are long gone.

If the consequences of pretending to know can be so damaging, why do people keep doing it?

That's easy: in most cases, the cost of saying "I don't know" is higher than the cost of being wrong—at least for the individual.

Think back to the soccer player who was about to take a life-changing penalty kick. Aiming toward the center has a better chance of success, but aiming toward a corner is less risky to his own reputation. So that's where he shoots. Every time we pretend to know something, we are doing the same: protecting our own reputation rather than promoting the collective good. None of us want to look stupid, or at least overmatched, by admitting we don't know an answer. The incentives to fake it are simply too strong.

Incentives can also explain why so many people are willing to predict the future. A huge payoff awaits anyone who makes a big and bold prediction that happens to come true. If you say the stock market will triple within twelve months and it actually does, you will be celebrated for years (and paid well for future predictions). What happens if the market crashes instead? No worries. Your prediction will already be forgotten. Since almost no one has a strong incentive to keep track of everyone else's bad predictions, it costs almost nothing to pretend you know what will happen in the future.

In 2011, an elderly Christian radio preacher named Harold Camping made headlines around the world by predicting that the Rapture would occur on Saturday, May 21 of that year. The world would end, he warned, and seven billion people—everyone but the hard-core believers—would die.

One of us has a young son who saw these headlines and got scared. His father reassured him that Camping's prediction was baseless, but the boy was distraught. In the nights leading up to May 21, he cried himself to sleep; it was a miserable experience for all. And then Saturday dawned bright and clear, the world still in one piece. The boy, with the false bravado of a ten-year-old, declared he'd never been scared at all.

"Even so," his father said, "what do you think should happen to Harold Camping?"

"Oh, that's easy," the boy said. "They should take him outside and shoot him."

This punishment may seem extreme, but the sentiment is understandable. When bad predictions are unpunished, what incentive is there to stop making them? One solution was recently proposed in Romania. That country boasts a robust population of "witches," women who tell fortunes for a living. Lawmakers decided that witches should be regulated, taxed, and—most important—made to pay a fine or even go to prison if the fortunes they told didn't prove accurate. The witches were understandably upset. One of them responded as she knew best: by threatening to cast a spell on the politicians with cat feces and a dog corpse.

There is one more explanation for why so many of us think we know more than we do. It has to do with something we all carry with us everywhere we go, even though we may not consciously think about it: a moral compass.

Each of us develops a moral compass (some stronger than others, to be sure) as we make our way through the world. This is for the most part a wonderful thing. Who wants to live in a world where people run around with no regard for the difference between right and wrong?

But when it comes to solving problems, one of the best ways to start is by putting away your moral compass.

Why?

When you are consumed with the rightness or wrongness of a given issue—whether it's fracking or gun control or genetically engineered food—it's easy to lose track of what the issue actually *is*. A moral compass can convince you that all the answers are obvious (even when they're not); that there is a bright line between right and wrong (when often there isn't); and, worst, that you are certain you already know everything you need to know about a subject so you stop trying to learn more.

In centuries past, sailors who relied on a ship's compass found it occasionally gave erratic readings that threw them off course. Why? The increasing use of metal on ships—iron nails and hardware, the sailors' tools and even their buckles and buttons—messed with the compass's magnetic read. Over time, sailors went to great lengths to keep metal from interfering with the compass. With such an evasive measure in mind, we are not suggesting you toss your moral compass in the trash—not at all—but only that you temporarily set it aside, to prevent it from clouding your vision.

Consider a problem like suicide. It is so morally fraught that we rarely discuss it in public; it is as if we've thrown a black drape over the entire topic.

This doesn't seem to be working out very well. There are about 38,000 suicides a year in the United States, more than twice the number of homicides. Suicide is one of the top ten causes of death for nearly every age group. Because talking about suicide carries such a strong moral taboo, these facts are little known.

As of this writing, the U.S. homicide rate is lower than it's been in fifty years. The rate of traffic fatalities is at a historic low, having fallen by two-thirds since the 1970s. The overall suicide rate, meanwhile, has barely budged—and worse yet, suicide among 15- to 24-year-olds has *tripled* over the past several decades.

One might think, therefore, that by studying the preponderance of cases, society has learned everything possible about what leads people to commit suicide.

David Lester, a psychology professor at Richard Stockton College in New Jersey, has likely thought about suicide longer, harder, and from more angles than any other human. In more than twenty-five-hundred academic publications, he has explored the relationship between suicide and, among other things, alcohol, anger, antidepressants, astrological signs, biochemistry, blood type, body type, depression, drug abuse, gun control, happiness, holidays, Internet use, IQ, mental illness, migraines, the moon, music, national-anthem lyrics, personality type, sexuality, smoking, spirituality, TV watching, and wide-open spaces.

Has all this study led Lester to some grand unified theory of suicide? Hardly. So far he has one compelling notion. It's what might be called the "no one left to blame" theory of suicide. While one might expect that suicide is highest among people whose lives are the hardest, research by Lester and others suggests the opposite: suicide is more common among people with a higher quality of life.

"If you're unhappy and you have something to blame your unhappiness on—if it's the government, or the economy, or something—then that kind of immunizes you against committing suicide," he says. "It's when you have *no* external cause to blame for your unhappiness that suicide becomes more likely. I've used this idea to explain why African-Americans have lower suicide rates, why blind people whose sight is restored often become suicidal, and why adolescent suicide rates often rise as their quality of life gets better."

That said, Lester admits that what he and other experts know about suicide is dwarfed by what is unknown. We don't know much, for instance, about the percentage of people who seek or get help before contemplating suicide. We don't know much about the "suicidal impulse"—how much time elapses between a person's decision and action. We don't even know what share of suicide victims are mentally ill. There is so much disagreement on this issue, Lester says, that estimates range from *5 percent to 94 percent*.

"I'm expected to know the answers to questions such as why people kill themselves," Lester says. "And myself and my friends, we often—when we're relaxing—admit that we really don't have a good idea why people kill themselves."

If someone like David Lester, one of the world's leading authorities in his field, is willing to admit how much he has to learn, shouldn't it be easier for all of us to do the same? All right, then: on to the learning.

The key to learning is feedback. It is nearly impossible to learn anything without it.

Imagine you're the first human in history who's trying to make bread—but you're not allowed to actually bake it and see how the recipe turns out. Sure, you can adjust the ingredients and other variables all you want. But if you never get to bake and eat the finished product, how will you know what works and what doesn't? Should the ratio of flour to water be 3:1 or 2:1? What happens if you add salt or oil or yeast—or maybe animal dung? Should the dough be left to sit before baking—and if so, for how long, and under what conditions? How long will it need to bake? Covered or uncovered? How hot should the fire be?

Even with good feedback, it can take a while to learn. (Just imagine how bad some of that early bread was!) But without it, you don't stand a chance; you'll go on making the same mistakes forever.

Thankfully, our ancestors did figure out how to bake bread, and since then we've learned to do all sorts of things: build a house, drive a car, write computer code, even figure out the kind of economic and social policies that voters like. Voting may be one of the sloppiest feedback loops around, but it is feedback nonetheless.

In a simple scenario, it's easy to gather feedback. When you're learning to drive a car, it's pretty obvious what happens when you take a sharp mountain curve at 80 miles an hour. (Hello, ravine!) But the more complex a problem is, the harder it is to capture good feedback. You can gather a lot of facts, and that may be helpful, but in order to reliably measure cause and effect you need to get beneath the facts. You may have to purposefully go out and create feedback through an experiment.

Not long ago, we met with some executives from a large multinational retailer. They were spending hundreds of millions of dollars a year on U.S. advertising—primarily TV commercials and print circulars in Sunday newspapers— but they weren't sure how effective it was. So far, they had come to one concrete conclusion: TV ads were about four times more effective, dollar for dollar, than print ads.

We asked how they knew this. They whipped out some beautiful, full-color PowerPoint charts that tracked the relationship between TV ads and product sales. Sure enough, there was a mighty sales spike every time their TV ads ran. Valuable feedback, right? Umm . . . let's make sure.

How often, we asked, did those ads air? The executives explained that because TV ads are so much more expensive than print ads, they were concentrated on just three days: Black Friday, Christmas, and Father's Day. In other words, the company spent millions of dollars to entice people to go shopping at precisely the same time that millions of people were about to go shopping anyway.

So how could they know the TV ads *caused* the sales spike? They couldn't! The causal relationship might just as easily move in the opposite direction, with the expected sales spike causing the company to buy TV ads. It's possible the company would have sold just as much merchandise without spending a single dollar on TV commercials. The feedback in this case was practically worthless.

Now we asked about the print ads. How often did they run? One executive told us, with obvious pride, that the company had bought newspaper inserts every single Sunday for the past twenty years in 250 markets across the United States.

So how could they tell whether *these* ads were effective? They couldn't. With no variation whatsoever, it was impossible to know.

What if, we said, the company ran an experiment to find out? In science, the randomized control trial has been the gold standard of learning for hundreds of years—but why should scientists have all the fun? We described an experiment the company might run. They could select 40 major markets across the country and randomly divide them into two groups. In the first group, the company would keep buying newspaper ads every Sunday. In the second group, they'd go totally dark—not a single ad. After three months, it would be easy to compare merchandise sales in the two groups to see how much the print ads mattered.

"Are you crazy?" one marketing executive said. "We can't possibly go dark in 20 markets. Our CEO would kill us."

"Yeah," said someone else, "it'd be like that kid in Pittsburgh."

What kid in Pittsburgh?

They told us about a summer intern who was supposed to call in the Sunday ad buys for the Pittsburgh newspapers. For whatever reason, he botched his assignment and failed to make the calls. So for the entire summer, the company ran no newspaper ads in a large chunk of Pittsburgh. "Yeah," one executive said, "we almost got fired for that one."

So what happened, we asked, to the company's Pittsburgh sales that summer?

They looked at us, then at each other—and sheepishly admitted it never occurred to them to check the data. When they went back and ran the numbers, they found something shocking: the ad blackout hadn't affected Pittsburgh sales at all!

Now *that,* we said, is valuable feedback. The company may well be wasting hundreds of millions of dollars on advertising. How could the executives know for sure? That 40-market experiment would go a long way toward answering the question. And so, we asked them, are you ready to try it now?

"Are you crazy?" the marketing executive said again. "We'll get fired if we do that!"

To this day, on every single Sunday in every single market, this company still buys newspaper advertising—even though the only real piece of feedback they ever got is that the ads *don't* work.

The experiment we proposed, while heretical to this company's executives, was nothing if not simple. It would have neatly allowed them to gather the feedback they needed. There is no guarantee they would have been happy with the result—maybe they'd need to spend *more* ad money, or maybe the ads were only successful in certain markets—but at least they would have gained a few clues as to what works and what doesn't. The miracle of a good experiment is that in one simple cut, you can eliminate all the complexity that makes it so hard to determine cause and effect.

But experimentation of this sort is regrettably rare in the corporate and nonprofit worlds, government, and elsewhere. Why?

One reason is tradition. In our experience, many institutions are used to making decisions based on some murky blend of gut instinct, moral compass, and whatever the previous decision maker did.

A second reason is lack of expertise: while it isn't hard to run a simple experiment, most people have never been taught to do so and may therefore be intimidated.

But there is a third, grimmer explanation for this general reluctance toward experimentation: it requires someone to say "I don't know." Why mess with an experiment when you think you already know the answer? Rather than waste time, you can just rush off and bankroll the project or pass the law without having to worry about silly details like whether or not it'll work.

If, however, you're willing to think like a Freak and admit what you don't know, you will see there is practically no limit to the power of a good randomized experiment.

Granted, not every scenario lends itself to experimentation, especially when it comes to social issues. In most places—in most democracies, at least—you can't just randomly select portions of the population and command them to, say, have 10 children instead of 2 or 3; or eat nothing but lentils for 20 years; or start going to church every day. That's why it pays to be on the lookout for a "natural experiment," a shock to the system that produces the sort of feedback you'd get if you *could* randomly command people to change their behavior.

A lot of the scenarios we've written about in our earlier books have exploited natural experiments. In trying to measure the knock-on effects of sending millions of people to prison, we took advantage of civil-rights lawsuits that forced overcrowded prisons in some states to set free thousands of inmates—something that no governor or mayor would voluntarily do. In analyzing the relationship between abortion and crime, we capitalized on the fact that the legalization of abortion was staggered in time across different states; this allowed us to better isolate its effects than if it had been legalized everywhere at once.

Alas, natural experiments as substantial as these are not common. One alternative is to set up a laboratory experiment. Social scientists around the world have been doing this in droves recently. They recruit legions of undergrads to act out various scenarios in the hopes of learning about everything from altruism to greed to criminality. Lab experiments can be incredibly useful in exploring behaviors that aren't so easy to capture in the real world. The results are often fascinating—but not necessarily that informative.

Why not? Most of them simply don't bear enough resemblance to the real-world scenarios they are trying to mimic. They are the academic equivalent of a marketing focus group—a small number of handpicked volunteers in an artificial environment who dutifully carry out the tasks requested by the person in charge. Lab experiments are invaluable in the hard sciences, in part because neutrinos and monads don't change their behavior when they are being watched; but humans do.

A better way to get good feedback is to run a field experiment—that is, rather than trying to mimic the real world in a lab, take the lab mind-set into the real world. You're still running an experiment but the subjects don't necessarily know it, which means the feedback you'll glean is pure.

With a field experiment, you can randomize to your heart's content, include more people than you could ever fit in a lab, and watch those people responding to real-world incentives rather than the encouragements of a professor hovering over them. When done well, field experiments can radically improve how problems get solved.

Already this is happening. In Chapter 6, you'll read about a clever field experiment that got homeowners in California to use less electricity, and another that helped a charity raise millions of dollars to help turn around the lives of poor children. In Chapter 9, we'll tell you about the most audacious experiment we've ever run, in which we recruited people facing hard life decisions—whether to join the military or quit a job or end a romantic relationship—and, with the flip of a coin, randomly made the decision for them.

• • •

As useful as experiments can be, there is one more reason a Freak might want to try them: it's fun! Once you embrace the spirit of experimentation, the world becomes a sandbox in which to try out new ideas, ask new questions, and challenge the prevailing orthodoxies.

You may have been struck, for example, by the fact that some wines are so much more expensive than others. Do expensive wines really taste better? Some years back, one of us tried an experiment to find out.

The setting was the Society of Fellows, a Harvard outpost where postdoctoral students carry out research and, once a week, sit with their esteemed elder Fellows for a formal dinner. Wine was a big part of these dinners, and the Society boasted a formidable cellar. It wasn't unusual for a bottle to cost $100. Our young Fellow wondered if this expense was justified. Several elder Fellows, who happened to be wine connoisseurs, assured him it was: an expensive bottle, they told him, was generally far superior to a cheaper version.

The young Fellow decided to run a blind tasting to see how true this was. He asked the Society's wine steward to pull two good vintages from the cellar. Then he went to a liquor store and bought the cheapest available bottle made from the same grape. It cost $8. He poured the three wines into four decanters, with one of the cellar wines repeated. Here was the layout:

DECANTER	WINE
1	EXPENSIVE WINE A
2	EXPENSIVE WINE B
3	CHEAP WINE
4	EXPENSIVE WINE A

When it came time to taste the wines, the elder Fellows couldn't have been more cooperative. They swirled, they sniffed, they sipped; they filled out marking cards, noting their assessment of each wine. They were not told that one of the wines cost about one-tenth the price of the others.

The results? On average, the four decanters received nearly identical ratings—that is, the cheap wine tasted just as good as the expensive ones. But that wasn't even the most surprising finding. The young Fellow also compared how each drinker rated each wine in comparison to the other wines. Can you guess which two decanters they judged as most different from each other? Decanters 1 and 4—which had been poured from the exact same bottle!

These findings were not greeted with universal good cheer. One of the elder connoisseur-Fellows loudly announced that he had a head cold, which presumably gummed up his palate, and stormed from the room.

Okay, so maybe this experiment wasn't very sporting—or scientific. Wouldn't it be nice to see the results of a more robust experiment along these lines?

Robin Goldstein, a food-and-wine critic who has studied

neuroscience, law, and French cuisine, decided to run such an experiment. Over several months, he organized 17 blind tastings across the United States that included more than 500 people, ranging from wine beginners to sommeliers and vintners.

Goldstein used 523 different wines, from $1.65 to $150 per bottle. The tastings were double-blind, meaning that neither the drinker nor the person serving the wine knew its identity or price. After each wine, a drinker would answer this question: "Overall, how do you find the wine?" The answers were "bad" (1 point), "okay" (2 points), "good" (3 points), and "great" (4 points).

The average rating for all wines, across all tasters, was 2.2, or just above "okay." So did the more expensive wines rack up more points? In a word: no. Goldstein found that on average, the people in his experiment "enjoy more expensive wines slightly *less*" than cheaper ones. He was careful to note that the experts in his sample—about 12 percent of the participants had some kind of wine training—did not prefer the cheaper wines, but nor was it clear that they preferred the expensive ones.

When you buy a bottle of wine, do you sometimes base your decision on how pretty the label is? According to Robin Goldstein's results, this doesn't seem like a bad strategy: at least it's easy to tell labels apart, unlike the stuff in the bottle.

Goldstein, already bound for heretic status in the wine

industry, had one more experiment to try. If more expensive wines don't taste better than cheap ones, he wondered, what about wine critics' ratings and awards—how legitimate are they? The best-known player in this arena is *Wine Spectator* magazine, which reviews thousands of wines and bestows its Award of Excellence to restaurants that serve "a well-chosen selection of quality producers, along with a thematic match to the menu in both price and style." Only a few thousand restaurants worldwide hold this distinction.

Goldstein wondered if the award is as meaningful as it seems. He created a fictional restaurant, in Milan, with a fake website and a fake menu, "a fun amalgamation of somewhat bumbling nouvelle-Italian recipes," he explained. He called it Osteria L'Intrepido, or "Fearless Restaurant," after his own *Fearless Critic* restaurant guides. "There were two questions being tested here," he says. "One was, do you have to have a good wine list to win a *Wine Spectator* Award of Excellence? And the second was, do you have to *exist* to win a *Wine Spectator* Award of Excellence?"

Goldstein took great care in creating L'Intrepido's fictional wine list, but not in the direction you might imagine. For the reserve list—typically a restaurant's best, most expensive wines—he chose wines that were particularly bad. The list included 15 wines that *Wine Spectator* itself had reviewed, using its 100-point scale. On this scale, anything above 90 is at least "outstanding"; above 80 is at least "good." If a wine gets 75–79 points, *Wine Spectator* calls it "mediocre." Anything below 74 is "not recommended."

So how had the magazine rated the 15 wines Goldstein chose for his reserve list? Their average *Wine Spectator* rating was a paltry 71. One vintage, according to *Wine Spectator*, "smells barnyardy and tastes decayed." Another had "just too much paint thinner and nail varnish character." A 1995 Cabernet Sauvignon "I Fossaretti," which scored a lowly 58 points, got this review from *Wine Spectator*: "Something wrong here . . . tasted metallic and odd." On Goldstein's reserve list, this bottle was priced at 120 euros; the average cost of the 15 bottles was about 180 euros.

How could Goldstein possibly expect that a fake restaurant whose most expensive wines had gotten terrible *Wine Spectator* reviews would win a *Wine Spectator* Award of Excellence?

"My hypothesis," he says, "was that the $250 fee was really the functional part of the application."

So he sent off the check, the application, and his wine list. Not long after, the answering machine at his fake restaurant in Milan received a real call from *Wine Spectator* in New York. He had won an Award of Excellence! The magazine also asked "if you might have an interest in publicizing your award with an ad in the upcoming issue." This led Goldstein to conclude that "the entire awards program was really just an advertising scheme."

Does that mean, we asked him, that the two of us—who

don't know a thing about running a restaurant—could some-day hope to win a *Wine Spectator* Award of Excellence?

"Yeah," he said, "if your wines are bad enough."

Maybe, you are thinking, it is obvious that "awards" like this are to some degree just a marketing stunt. Maybe it was also obvious to you that more expensive wines don't necessarily taste better or that a lot of advertising money is wasted.

But a lot of obvious ideas are only obvious after the fact—after someone has taken the time and effort to inves-tigate them, to prove them right (or wrong). The impulse to investigate can only be set free if you stop pretending to know answers that you don't. Because the incentives to pre-tend are so strong, this may require some bravery on your part.

Remember those British schoolchildren who made up answers about Mary's trip to the seashore? The researchers who ran that experiment did a follow-up study, called "Help-ing Children Correctly Say 'I Don't Know' to Unanswerable Questions." Once again, the children were asked a series of questions; but in this case, they were explicitly told to say "I don't know" if a question was unanswerable. The happy news is that the children were wildly successful at saying "I don't know" when appropriate, while still getting the other questions right.

Let us all take encouragement from the kids' progress. The next time you run into a question that you can only pretend to answer, go ahead and say "I don't know"—and then follow up, certainly, with "but maybe I can find out." And work as hard as you can to do that. You may be surprised by how receptive people are to your confession, especially when you come through with the real answer a day or a week later.

But even if this goes poorly—if your boss sneers at your ignorance or you can't figure out the answer no matter how hard you try—there is another, more strategic benefit to occasionally saying "I don't know." Let's say you've already done that on a few occasions. The next time you're in a real jam, facing an important question that you just can't answer, go ahead and make up something—and everyone will believe you, because you're the guy who all those other times was crazy enough to admit you didn't know the answer.

After all, just because you're at the office is no reason to stop thinking.

CHAPTER 3

What's Your Problem?

If it takes a lot of courage to admit you don't know all the answers, just imagine how hard it is to admit you don't even know the right question. But if you ask the wrong question, you are almost guaranteed to get the wrong answer.

Think about a problem you'd really like to see solved. The obesity epidemic, perhaps, or climate change or the decline of the American public-school system. Now ask yourself how you came to define the problem as you see it. In all likelihood, your view was heavily influenced by the popular press.

Most people don't have the time or inclination to think very hard about big problems like this. We tend to pay attention to what other people say and, if their views resonate with us, we slide our perception atop theirs. Furthermore, we tend to focus on the part of a problem that *bothers* us.

Maybe you hate the idea of substandard schools because your grandmother was a teacher and she seemed so much more devoted to education than today's teachers. To you, it is obvious that schools are failing because there are too many bad teachers.

Let's consider this a bit more closely. In the U.S. push for education reform, theories abound as to the key factors: school size, class size, administrative stability, money for technology, and, yes, teacher skill. It is demonstrably true that a good teacher is better than a bad teacher, and it is also true that overall teacher quality has fallen since your grandmother's day, in part because smart women now have so many more job options. Furthermore, in some countries—Finland and Singapore and South Korea, for instance—future schoolteachers are recruited from the best college-bound students, whereas a teacher in the United States is more likely to come from the bottom half of her class. So perhaps it makes sense that every conversation about school reform should focus on teacher skill.

But a mountain of recent evidence suggests that teacher skill has less influence on a student's performance than a completely different set of factors: namely, how much kids have learned from their parents, how hard they work at home, and whether the parents have instilled an appetite for education. If these home-based inputs are lacking, there is only so much a school can do. Schools have your kid for only seven hours a day, 180 days a year, or about 22 percent of the child's waking hours. Nor is all that time devoted to learning, once you account for socializing and eating and getting to and from class. And for many kids, the first three or four years of life is all parents and no school.

But when serious people talk about education reform, they rarely talk about the family's role in preparing children to succeed. That is in part because the very words "education reform" indicate that the question is "What's wrong with our schools?" when in reality, the question might be better phrased as "Why do American kids know less than kids from Estonia and Poland?" When you ask the question differently, you look for answers in different places.

So maybe, when we talk about why American kids aren't doing so well, we should be talking less about schools and more about parents.

In our society, if someone wants to be a hairstylist or a kickboxer or a hunting guide—or a schoolteacher—he or she must be trained and licensed by a state agency. No such requirement is necessary for parenthood. Anyone with a set of reproductive organs is free to create a child, no questions asked, and raise them as they see fit, so long as there are no visible bruises—and then turn that child over to the school system so the teachers can work their magic. Maybe we are asking too much of the schools and too little of our parents and kids?

Here is the broader point: whatever problem you're trying to solve, make sure you're not just attacking the noisy part of the problem that happens to capture your attention. Before spending all your time and resources, it's incredibly important to properly define the problem—or, better yet, *re*define the problem.

That is what an unassuming Japanese college student did when he took on the sort of challenge most of us wouldn't dream about—or even want to.

In the autumn of 2000, a young man who would come to be known as Kobi was studying economics at Yokkaichi University, in Mie prefecture. He lived with his girlfriend, Kumi. They lit the apartment by candle since they could no longer afford the electricity bill. Neither of them came from a family of significant means—Kobi's father was a disciple at a Buddhist temple, giving tours about its history—and they were behind on the rent as well.

Kumi heard about a contest that paid $5,000 to the winner. Without telling Kobi, she sent in a postcard to sign him up. It was a televised eating competition.

This was far from an obviously good idea. Kobi wasn't gluttonous in the least; he had a slight build and stood barely five foot eight. He did, however, have a strong stomach and a good appetite. As a child, he had always cleaned his plate and sometimes his sisters' plates too. He also believed that size could be overrated. One of his childhood heroes was the great sumo champion Chiyonofuji, a.k.a. the Wolf, who was relatively light but compensated with superior technique.

Kobi reluctantly agreed to enter the contest. His only

chance was to outthink the competition. At university, he had been learning about game theory and now it came in handy. The contest would have four stages: boiled potatoes followed by a seafood bowl, Mongolian mutton barbecue, and noodles. Only the top finishers from each stage would advance. Kobi studied earlier multistage eating contests. He saw that most competitors went so hard in the early rounds that even if they did advance, they were too exhausted (and stuffed) to do well in the finals. His strategy was to conserve energy and stomach capacity by eating just enough at each stage to qualify for the next. It wasn't exactly rocket science, but then his competitors weren't rocket scientists either. In the final round, Kobi channeled his boyhood sumo hero and wolfed down enough noodles to win the $5,000 prize. The lights went back on in Kobi and Kumi's apartment.

There was more money to be made in Japanese eating contests but Kobi, having tasted amateur success, was eager to go pro. He set his sights on the Super Bowl of competitive eating, as the sport is known: the Nathan's Famous Fourth of July International Hot Dog Eating Contest. For some four decades it has been held at Coney Island in New York City—the *New York Times* and others have written the contest goes back to 1916, but its promoters admit they concocted that history—and it routinely draws more than one million viewers on ESPN.

The rules were simple. A contestant ate as many hot dogs and buns ("HDB," officially) as he could in 12 minutes. Any HDB or portion thereof already in the eater's mouth when the final bell rang would count toward his total as long as he swallowed it eventually. An eater could be disqualified, however, if during the contest a significant amount of HDB that had gone into his mouth came back out—known in the sport as a "reversal of fortune." Condiments were allowed but no serious competitor would bother. Beverages were also allowed, any kind in unlimited quantity. In 2001, when Kobi decided to enter the Coney Island contest, the record stood at a mind-boggling 25⅛ HDB in 12 minutes.

At home in Japan, he practiced. He had a hard time finding regulation hot dogs, so he used sausages made from minced fish. Instead of buns, he cut up loaves of bread. For months, he trained in obscurity, and he arrived at Coney Island in obscurity as well. A year earlier, the top three finishers were all Japanese—Kazutoyo "the Rabbit" Arai held the world record—but this newcomer was not considered a threat. Some thought he was a high-school student, which would have made him ineligible. One contestant mocked him: "Your legs are thinner than my arms!"

How did he do? In his very first Coney Island contest, Kobi smoked the field and set a new world record. How many hot dogs and buns would you guess he ate? The record, remember, was 25⅛. A sensible guess might be 27 or even 28 HDB. That would be more than a 10 percent gain over the old record. If you wanted to make a really aggressive guess, you might suppose a 20 percent gain, which would mean a bit more than 30 HDB in 12 minutes.

But he ate 50. Fifty! That's more than four hot dogs

and buns per minute for 12 straight minutes. The slender twenty-three-year-old Kobi—full name Takeru Kobayashi—had essentially *doubled* the world record.

Just think about that margin of victory. The Coney Island hot-dog contest isn't as historically significant as, say, the 100-meter dash, but let's put Kobayashi's feat in perspective. The 100-meter record is as of this writing held by Usain Bolt, the Jamaican sprinter with the perfect name, at 9.58 seconds. Even in such a brief race, Bolt often beats his rivals by a few strides; he is widely considered the best sprinter in history. Before Bolt, the record was 9.74 seconds. So his improvement was 1.6 percent. If he had treated that record as Kobayashi treated his, Usain Bolt would have run the 100 meters in about 4.87 seconds, for an average speed of roughly 46 miles per hour. That's somewhere between a greyhound and a cheetah.

Kobayashi won Coney Island again the following year, and the next four years too, pushing the record to 53¾ HDB. No past champion had won more than three times, much less six in a row. But it wasn't just the winning or the margin of victory that set him apart. The typical competitive eater looked as if he could gobble down Kobayashi himself; he was the kind of man famous in his fraternity house for consuming two entire pizzas and a six-pack at one sitting. Kobayashi, meanwhile, was soft-spoken, playful, and analytical.

He became an international superstar. In Japan, the enthusiasm for eating contests cooled after a schoolboy choked to death imitating his heroes. But Kobayashi found plenty of competition elsewhere, setting records in hamburgers, bratwurst, Twinkies, lobster rolls, fish tacos, and more. A rare defeat came in a one-on-one TV event. In roughly 2.5 minutes, Kobayashi ate 31 bunless hot dogs, but his opponent ate 50. The opponent was a half-ton Kodiak bear.

Initially, his dominance at Coney Island was perplexing. Some rivals thought he was cheating. Perhaps he took a muscle relaxant or some other foreign substance to quell the gag reflex? He was rumored to have swallowed stones to expand his stomach. There were even whispers that Kobayashi represented a Japanese government plot to humiliate the Americans—at a contest held on Independence Day, no less!—and that Japanese doctors had surgically implanted a second esophagus or stomach.

Alas, none of these charges seem to be true. So why *was* Takeru Kobayashi so much better than everyone else?

We met with him on several occasions to try to answer that question. The first meeting took place one summer evening in New York, over dinner at Cafe Luxembourg, a quietly chic restaurant on the Upper West Side. Kobayashi ate daintily— a small green salad, English breakfast tea, a bit of duck breast with no sauce. It was hard to imagine he was the same person who crammed so many hot dogs in his mouth when the bell rang; it was like watching a cage fighter doing needlepoint. "Compared to the American eaters," he says,

"I don't eat very much regularly. To eat quickly is not very good manners. Everything I do is against the manners and morals of Japanese people."

His mother did not care for his chosen profession. "I would never talk to her about my contests or the training." But in 2006, when she was dying of cancer, she seemed to draw inspiration from it. "She was taking the chemotherapy, so she would want to throw up a lot. And she would say, 'You're also fighting the urge to throw up from eating so much, so I feel like I can try and sustain.'"

His features are delicate—soft eyes and high cheekbones that give him a spritely look. His hair is cut stylishly and dyed, red on one side and yellow on the other, representing ketchup and mustard. He begins to speak, quietly but intensely, about how he trained for his first Coney Island competition. Those months in isolation, it turned out, were one long bout of experimentation and feedback.

Kobayashi had observed that most Coney Island eaters used a similar strategy, which was not really much of a strategy at all. It was essentially a sped-up version of how the average person eats a hot dog at a backyard barbecue: pick it up, cram the dog and bun into the mouth, chew from end to end, and glug some water to wash it down. Kobayashi wondered if perhaps there was a better way.

Nowhere was it written, for instance, that the dog must be eaten end to end. His first experiment was simple: What would happen if he broke the dog and bun in half before eating? This, he found, afforded more options for chewing and loading, and it also let his hands do some of the work that would otherwise occupy his mouth. This maneuver would come to be known as the Solomon Method, after the biblical King Solomon, who settled a maternity dispute by threatening to slice a baby into two pieces (more on that later, in Chapter 7).

Kobayashi now questioned another conventional practice: eating the dog and bun together. It wasn't surprising that everyone did this. The dog is nested so comfortably in the bun, and when eating for pleasure, the soft blandness of the bun pairs wonderfully with the slick, seasoned meat. But Kobayashi wasn't eating for pleasure. Chewing dog and bun together, he discovered, created a density conflict. The dog itself is a compressed tube of dense, salty meat that can practically slide down the gullet on its own. The bun, while airy and less substantial, takes up a lot of space and requires a lot of chewing.

So he started removing the dog from bun. Now he could feed himself a handful of bunless dogs, broken in half, followed by a round of buns. He was like a one-man factory, working toward the kind of specialization that has made economists' hearts beat faster since the days of Adam Smith.

As easily as he was able to swallow the hot dogs—like a trained dolphin *slorp*ing down herring at the aquarium— the bun was still a problem. (If you want to win a bar bet, challenge someone to eat two hot-dog buns in one minute without a beverage; it is nearly impossible.) So Kobayashi tried something different. As he was feeding himself the bunless, broken hot dogs with one hand, he used the other hand to dunk the bun into his water cup. Then he'd squeeze out most of the excess water and smush the bun into his mouth. This might seem counterintuitive—why put extra liquid in your stomach when you need all available space for buns and dogs?—but the bun-dunking provided a hidden benefit. Eating soggy buns meant Kobayashi grew less thirsty along the way, which meant less time wasted on drinking. He experimented with water temperature and found that warm was best, as it relaxed his chewing muscles. He also spiked the water with vegetable oil, which seemed to help swallowing.

His experimentation was endless. He videotaped his training sessions and recorded all his data in a spreadsheet, hunting for inefficiencies and lost milliseconds. He experimented with pace: Was it better to go hard the first four minutes, ease off during the middle four, and "sprint" toward the end—or maintain a steady pace throughout? (A fast start, he discovered, was best.) He found that getting a lot of sleep was especially important. So was weight training: strong muscles aided in eating and helped resist the urge to throw up. He also discovered that he could make more room in his stomach by jumping and wriggling as he ate—a strange, animalistic dance that came to be known as the Kobayashi Shake.

Just as important as the tactics he adopted were those he rejected. Unlike other competitive eaters, he never trained at an all-you-can-eat restaurant. ("If I do that, I don't know how much of what I ate.") He did not listen to music while eating. ("I don't want to hear any extra sounds.") He found that drinking gallons of water could expand his stomach, but the end result was disastrous. ("I started to have a sort of seizure, like an epileptic seizure. So that was a big mistake.")

When he put it all together, Kobayashi found that his physical preparations could produce an elevated mental state. "In ordinary cases, eating so much for ten minutes— the last two minutes are the toughest moments, and you worry. But if you have great concentration, then it's enjoyable. You feel pain and suffering—however, as you feel it, you feel more excited. And that's when highness is upon you."

But wait a minute. What if Kobayashi, for all his methodological innovation, was simply an anatomical freak, a once-in-a-lifetime eating machine?

The best evidence against this argument is that his competition began to catch up with him. After six years of domination at Coney Island, Kobayashi was overtaken by the American eater Joey "Jaws" Chestnut, who went on to win *seven* straight Coney Island contests as of this writing.

Often, he beat Kobayashi by just a whisker. The two of them pushed the world record ever upward, with Chestnut scarfing a mind-boggling 69 HDB in just 10 minutes (the contest was shortened by two minutes in 2008). Meanwhile, a handful of rivals—including Patrick "Deep Dish" Bertoletti and Tim "Eater X" Janus—routinely eat more HDB than Kobayashi did when he first doubled the old record. So does the female record holder, 98-pound Sonya "the Black Widow" Thomas, who has eaten 45 HDB in 10 minutes. Some of Kobayashi's rivals have copied certain strategies of his. All of them gained from the knowledge that 40 or 50 HDB, once considered a fantasy, plainly isn't.

In 2010, Kobayashi got into a contract dispute with the organizers of the Coney Island event—he claimed they limited his ability to compete elsewhere—and he wasn't in the lineup. But he showed up anyway and, in the excitement, jumped onstage. He was promptly handcuffed and arrested. It was an uncharacteristically brash move for such a disciplined man. That night in jail, he was given a sandwich and milk. "I am very hungry," he said. "I wish there were hot dogs in jail."

Can the success of Takeru Kobayashi, as magnificent as it was, be applied to anything more significant than the high-speed consumption of hot dogs? We believe it can. If you think like a Freak, there are at least two broader lessons to be gleaned from his approach.

The first is about problem solving generally. Kobayashi redefined the problem he was trying to solve. What question were his competitors asking? It was essentially: *How do I eat more hot dogs?* Kobayashi asked a different question: *How do I make hot dogs easier to eat?* This question led him to experiment and gather the feedback that changed the game. Only by redefining the problem was he able to discover a new set of solutions.

Kobayashi came to view competitive eating as a fundamentally different activity than everyday eating. He saw it as a sport—a disgusting one, perhaps, at least to most people—but, as with any sport, it required specific training, strategy, and physical and mental maneuvers. Seeing an eating contest as an amplified version of everyday eating was, to him, like seeing a marathon as an amplified version of walking down the street. Sure, most of us walk well enough, and even for a long time if necessary. But completing a marathon is a bit more complicated than that.

It is of course easier to redefine a problem like competitive eating than, say, a faltering education system or endemic poverty—but even with complex issues like these, a good start would be to assess the core of the problem as shrewdly as Kobayashi did with his.

The second lesson to be drawn from Kobayashi's success has to do with the limits that we accept, or refuse to.

Over dinner that night at Cafe Luxembourg, Kobayashi said that when he started training, he refused to acknowledge the legitimacy of the existing Coney Island record of 25⅛ HDB. Why? He reasoned that the record didn't stand for much since his earlier competitors had been asking the wrong question about eating hot dogs. As he saw it, the record was an artificial barrier.

So he went into the contest not thinking about 25⅛ as any sort of an upper bound. He instructed his mind to pay zero attention to the number of dogs he was eating and to concentrate solely on how he ate them. Would he still have won that first contest if he had mentally honored the barrier of 25⅛? Perhaps, but it is hard to imagine he would have *doubled* the record.

In recent experiments, scientists have found that even elite athletes can be tricked into improvement by essentially lying to them. In one experiment, cyclists were told to pedal a stationary bike at top speed for the equivalent of 4,000 meters. Later they repeated the task while watching an avatar of themselves pedaling in the earlier time trial. What the cyclists didn't know was that the researchers had turned up the speed on the avatar. And yet the cyclists were able to keep up with their avatars, surpassing what they thought had been their top speed. "It is the brain, not the heart or lungs, that is the critical organ," said the esteemed neurologist Roger Bannister, best known as the first human to run the mile in less than four minutes.

All of us face barriers—physical, financial, temporal— every day. Some are unquestionably real. But others are plainly artificial—expectations about how well a given system can function, or how much change is too much, or what kinds of behaviors are acceptable. The next time you encounter such a barrier, imposed by people who lack your imagination and drive and creativity, think hard about ignoring it. Solving a problem is hard enough; it gets that much harder if you've decided beforehand it can't be done.

If you doubt the adverse power of artificial limits, here's a simple test. Let's say you haven't been exercising and want to get back in the groove. You decide to do some push-ups. How many? *Well, it's been a while,* you tell yourself, *let me start with 10.* Down you go. When do you start getting mentally and physically tired? Probably around push-up number 7 or 8.

Imagine now that you had decided on 20 push-ups instead of 10. When do you start getting tired this time? Go ahead, hit the floor and try it. You probably blasted right past 10 before you even remembered how out of shape you are.

It was by refusing to accept the existing hot-dog record that Kobayashi blasted right through number 25 that first year. At Coney Island, each eater was assigned a Bunnette, a young woman who held aloft a signboard to show the audience each eater's progress. That year, the signboards didn't go high enough. Kobi's Bunnette had to hold up plain sheets of yellow paper with hastily scribbled numbers. When it was all over, a Japanese TV reporter asked him how he felt.

"I can keep going," Kobi said.

CHAPTER 4

Like a Bad Dye Job, the Truth Is in the Roots

It takes a truly original thinker to look at a problem that everyone else has already looked at and find a new avenue of attack.

Why is this so rare? Perhaps because most of us, when trying to figure out a problem, gravitate toward the nearest and most obvious cause. It's hard to say whether this is learned behavior or if it dates to our distant past.

In the caveman era, it was a matter of life or death to know if the berries on a particular bush were edible. The proximate cause was usually the one that mattered. Even today, the most proximate cause often makes perfect sense. If your three-year-old child is wailing and your five-year-old is standing nearby with a devilish grin and a plastic hammer, it's a good bet the hammer had something to do with the wailing.

But the big problems that society cares about—crime and disease and political dysfunction, for instance—are more complicated than that. Their root causes are often not so nearby, or obvious, or palatable. So rather than address their root causes, we often spend billions of dollars treating the symptoms and are left to grimace when the problem remains. Thinking like a Freak means you should work terribly hard to identify and attack the root cause of problems.

Of course this is far more easily said than done. Consider poverty and famine: What causes them? A glib answer is the lack of money and food. So theoretically you can fight poverty and famine by airlifting vast amounts of money and food into poor and hungry places.

That is pretty much what governments and aid groups have been doing for many years. So why do the same problems persist in the same places?

Because poverty is a symptom—of the absence of a workable economy built on credible political, social, and legal institutions. It's hard to fix that even with planeloads of cash. Similarly, the lack of food is usually not the root cause of famine. "Starvation is the characteristic of some people not *having* enough food to eat," the economist Amartya Sen wrote in his landmark book *Poverty and Famines*. "It is not the characteristic of there *being* not enough food to eat." In countries whose political and economic institutions are built to serve the appetites of a corrupt few rather than the multitudes, food is routinely withheld from the people who need it most. In the United States, meanwhile, we throw away an astonishing 40 percent of the food we buy.

Alas, fixing corruption is a lot harder than airlifting food. So even when you *do* get to the root cause of the problem, you may still be stuck. But as we'll see in this chapter, the stars occasionally align and the payoff can be huge.

In *Freakonomics,* we examined the causes of the rise and fall in violent crime in the United States. In 1960, crime began a sudden climb. By 1980, the homicide rate had doubled, reaching a historic peak. For several years crime stayed perilously high but in the early 1990s, it began to fall and kept falling.

So what happened?

A great many explanations were put forth, and in our book we put a number of them under empirical scrutiny. Below are two sets of possible explanations. One had a strong impact on lowering crime and one did not. Can you guess which is which?

A.	B.
Tighter gun laws	More police officers
A surging economy	More people sent to prison
More capital punishment	The decline of the crack-cocaine market

Each set is quite plausible, isn't it? Indeed, until you roll up your sleeves and crunch some data, it is virtually impossible to know the right answer.

So what do the data say?

The A factors, as logical as they may seem, did not contribute to the crime drop. Maybe this surprises you. Gun murders are down? *Well*, you figure, *that must be from all those tough new gun laws*—until you examine the data and find that most people who commit crimes with guns are almost entirely unaffected by current gun laws.

You might also think the go-go economy of the 1990s would have helped, but historical data show there is a surprisingly weak relationship between economic cycles and violent crime. Indeed, as the Great Recession took hold in 2007, a chorus of pundits warned that our long, lovely reprieve from violent crime was over. But it wasn't. Between 2007 and 2010, the worst years of the recession, homicide fell an additional 16 percent. The homicide rate today is, improbably, lower than it was in 1960.

The B factors, meanwhile—more cops, more people in prison, and a collapsing crack market—*did* contribute to the crime drop. But once we tallied up the cumulative impact of these factors, they still couldn't account for the entire crime drop. There had to be something else.

Let's take a closer look at the B factors. Do they address the root causes of crime? Not really. They might more plausibly be called present-tense factors. Sure, hiring more cops and putting more people in prison may shrink the short-term supply of criminals, but what about the long-term supply?

In *Freakonomics,* we identified one missing factor: the legalization of abortion in the early 1970s. The theory was jarring but simple. A rise in abortion meant that fewer unwanted children were being born, which meant fewer children growing up in the sort of difficult circumstances that increase the likelihood of criminality.

Given the history of abortion in the U.S.—there are few issues as morally and politically fraught—this theory was bound to be discomfiting for abortion opponents and supporters alike. We steeled ourselves for a shouting match.

Interestingly, our argument didn't generate much hate mail. Why? Our best guess is that readers were smart enough to understand that we had identified abortion as a mechanism for the crime drop but not the actual root cause. So what is the root cause? Simply this: too many children were being brought up in bad environments that led them to crime. As the first post-abortion generation came of age, it included fewer children who'd been raised in such environments.

It can be unsettling, even frightening, to stare a root cause in the eye. Maybe that's why we so often avoid it. It is a lot easier to argue about cops and prisons and gun laws than the thorny question of what makes a parent fit to raise a child. But if you want to have a worthwhile conversation about crime, it makes sense to start by talking about the benefits of good, loving parents who give their children a chance to lead safe and productive lives.

That may not be a simple conversation. But when you are dealing with root causes, at least you know you are fighting the real problem and not just boxing with shadows.

It may seem daunting to travel backward a generation or two in order to understand the root cause of a problem. But in some cases, a generation is barely the blink of an eye.

Let's pretend you are a German factory worker. You're sitting in a beer hall with friends after a shift, demoralized by your financial standing. The national economy is humming along, but it seems as if you and everyone else in town is running in place. The people who live just a few towns over, meanwhile, are doing considerably better. Why?

To find out, we must travel all the way back to the sixteenth century. In 1517, a distraught young German priest named Martin Luther levied a list of ninety-five grievances against the Roman Catholic Church. One practice he found particularly odious was the sale of indulgences—that is, the Church's practice of raising cash by forgiving the sins of big-ticket donors. (One senses that today Luther would rail against the tax treatment enjoyed by hedge funds and private-equity firms.)

Luther's bold move launched the Protestant Reformation. Germany at the time was made up of more than one thousand independent territories, each ruled by its own prince or duke. Some of these men followed Luther and embraced Protestantism; others stayed loyal to the Church. This schism would play out for decades all over Europe, often with immense bloodshed. In 1555, a temporary settlement was reached, the Peace of Augsburg, which allowed each German prince to freely select the religion to be practiced in his territory. Moreover, if a Catholic family lived in a territory whose prince chose Protestantism, the Peace allowed them to freely migrate to a Catholic area, and vice versa.

And so it was that Germany became a religious patchwork. Catholicism remained popular in the southeast and northwest while Protestantism took off in the central and northeast regions; other areas were mixed.

Fast-forward some 460 years to today. A young economist named Jörg Spenkuch discovered that if he laid a map of modern Germany over a map of sixteenth-century Germany, he could see that the religious patchwork was largely intact. The old Protestant areas are still largely Protestant while the old Catholic areas are still largely Catholic (except for the former East Germany, which took on a lot of atheism during its Communist period). The choices the princes made centuries ago still hold sway.

Perhaps this isn't so surprising. Germany, after all, is a nation steeped in tradition. But Spenkuch, while playing around with those maps, found something that *did* surprise him. The religious patchwork of modern Germany also overlapped with an interesting economic patchwork: the people living in Protestant areas earned more money than those in Catholic areas. Not a great deal more—about 1 percent—but the difference was clear. If the prince in your area had sided with the Catholics, you were likely to be poorer today than if he had followed Martin Luther.

How to explain this income patchwork? There could of course be present-tense reasons. Perhaps the higher earners got more education, or had better marriages, or lived closer to the high-paying jobs found in big cities.

But Spenkuch analyzed the relevant data and found that none of these factors could account for the income gap. Only one factor could: religion itself. He concluded that the people in Protestant areas make more money than the people in Catholic areas simply because they are Protestants!

Why? Was some kind of religious cronyism to blame, with Protestant bosses giving better jobs to Protestant workers? Apparently not. In fact, the data showed that Protestants don't earn higher hourly wages than Catholics—and yet they do manage to have higher incomes overall. So how does Spenkuch explain the Protestant-Catholic income gap?

He identified three factors:

1. Protestants tend to work a few more hours per week than Catholics.

2. Protestants are more likely than Catholics to be self-employed.

3. Protestant women are more likely than Catholic women to work full-time.

It appears that Jörg Spenkuch found living proof of the Protestant work ethic. That was the theory put forth in the early 1900s by the German sociologist Max Weber, which argued that capitalism took off in Europe in part because Protestants embraced the earthly notion of hard work as part of their divine mission.

So what does all this mean for the disgruntled factory worker drowning his economic sorrows in the beer hall? Unfortunately, not much. For him, it's probably too late unless he wants to shake up his life and start working harder. But at least he can push his kids to follow the lead of the hardworking Protestants a few towns over.*

Once you start looking at the world through a long lens, you will find many examples of contemporary behaviors that are driven by root causes from centuries past.

Why, for instance, are some Italian towns more likely than others to participate in civic and philanthropic programs? Because, as some researchers argue, during the Middle Ages these towns were free city-states rather than areas ruled by Norman overlords. Such an independent history apparently fosters a lasting trust in civic institutions.

---

* In defense, however, of Germanic Catholicism: a new research project by Spenkuch argues that Protestants were roughly twice as likely as Catholics to vote for the Nazis.

In Africa, some countries that regained independence from their colonial rulers have experienced brutal wars and rampant corruption; others haven't. Why? One pair of scholars found an answer that goes back many years. When the European powers began their mad "Scramble for Africa" in the nineteenth century, they carved up existing territories by looking at maps from afar. When creating new borders, they considered two essential criteria: land mass and water. The actual Africans who lived in these territories were not a major concern for the colonialists, since to them one African looked pretty much like the next one.

This method might make sense if you are cutting a cherry pie. But a continent is more problematic. These new colonial borders often split up large, harmonious ethnic groups. Suddenly, some members of the group became residents of one new country; others, a second country—along with, often, members of a *different* ethnic group with whom the first group wasn't so harmonious. Ethnic strife tended to be tamped down by colonial rule, but when the Europeans eventually returned to Europe, the African countries where unfriendly ethnic groups had been artificially jumbled were far more likely to devolve into war.

The scars of colonialism still haunt South America as well. Spanish conquistadors who found silver or gold in Peru, Bolivia, and Colombia would enslave the locals to work in the mines. What kind of long-term effect did this have? As several economists have found, people in those mining areas are to this day poorer than their neighbors, and their children are less likely to be vaccinated or get an education.

There is another case—a bizarre one, to be sure—in which the long arm of slavery reaches across history. Roland Fryer, an economist at Harvard, is consumed with closing the gap between blacks and whites in education, income, and health. Not long ago, he set out to understand why whites outlive blacks by several years. One thing was clear: heart disease, historically the biggest killer of both whites and blacks, is far more common among blacks. But why?

Fryer crunched all sorts of numbers. But he found that none of the obvious stressors—diet, smoking, even poverty—could account for the entire gap.

Then he found something that might. Fryer happened upon an old illustration called "An Englishman Tastes the Sweat of an African." It showed a slave trader in West Africa who appeared to be licking the slave's face.

Why would he do that?

One possibility was that he was somehow screening the slave for illness, not wanting to contaminate the rest of his cargo. Fryer wondered if the slave trader was perhaps testing the slave's "saltiness." That, after all, is what sweat tastes like. If so, why—and might this answer inform the broader agenda Fryer was pursuing?

The ocean journey of a slave from Africa to America was long and gruesome; many slaves died en route. Dehydration was a major cause. Who, Fryer wondered, is less likely to suffer from dehydration? Someone with a high degree of salt sensitivity. That is, if you are able to retain more salt, you will also retain more water—and be less likely to die during the Middle Passage. So perhaps the slave trader in the illustration wanted to find the saltier slaves in order to ensure his investment.

Fryer, who is black, mentioned this theory to a Harvard colleague, David Cutler, a prominent health economist who is white. Cutler at first thought it was "absolutely crazy," but upon deeper inspection it made sense. Indeed, some earlier medical research made a similar claim, although it was in considerable dispute.

Fryer began to fit the pieces together. "You might think anyone who could survive a voyage like this would be very fit and therefore would have a longer life expectancy," he says. "But actually this peculiar selection mechanism says that you can survive an ordeal such as the Middle Passage, but it's horrible for hypertension and related diseases. And salt sensitivity is a highly heritable trait, meaning that your descendants, i.e., black Americans, stand a pretty good chance of being hypertensive or of having cardiovascular disease."

Fryer looked for further evidence that might support his theory. American blacks are about 50 percent more likely to have hypertension than American whites. Again, this could be due to differences like diet and income. So what did the hypertension rates of *other* black populations look like? Fryer found that among Caribbean blacks—another population brought from Africa as slaves—hypertension rates were also elevated. But he noted that blacks who still live in Africa are statistically indistinguishable from whites in America. The evidence was hardly conclusive, but Fryer was convinced that the selection mechanism of the slave trade could be a long-lasting root cause of African-Americans' higher mortality rates.

As you can imagine, Fryer's theory isn't universally popular. Many people are uncomfortable talking about genetic racial difference at all. "People e-mail me and say, 'Can't you see the slippery slope here!? Can you see the perils of this argument?'"

Fresh medical research may prove that the salt-sensitivity theory isn't even right. But if it is, even in small measure, the potential benefits are huge. "There's something that can be done," Fryer says. "A diuretic that helps your body get rid of your salts. A little common pill."

· · ·

You might think that medicine, with such strong doses of science and logic, is one field in which root causes are always well understood.

Alas, you would be wrong. The human body is a complex, dynamic system about which a great deal remains unknown. Writing as recently as 1997, the medical historian Roy Porter put it this way: "We live in an age of science, but science has not eliminated fantasies about health; the stigmas of sickness, the moral meanings of medicine continue." As a result, gut hunches are routinely passed off as dogma while conventional wisdom flourishes even when there is no data to back it up.

Consider the ulcer. It is essentially a hole in your stomach or small intestine, producing a searing and surging pain. By the early 1980s, the causes of an ulcer were said to be definitively known: they were inherited or caused by psychological stress and spicy food, either of which could produce an overabundance of stomach acid. To anyone who has ever eaten a pile of jalapeños, this seems plausible. And as any doctor could attest, a patient with a bleeding ulcer was likely to be stressed out. (A doctor might just as easily note that shooting victims tend to bleed a lot, but that doesn't mean the blood caused the gunshot.)

Since the causes of ulcers were known, so too was the treatment. Patients were advised to relax (to cut down on stress), drink milk (to soothe the stomach), and take a Zantac or Tagamet pill (to block the production of stomach acid).

How well did this work?

To put it charitably: so-so. The treatment did help manage

a patient's pain, but the condition wasn't cured. And an ulcer is more than a painful nuisance. It can easily become fatal due to peritonitis (caused by a hole going clear through the stomach wall) or complications from bleeding. Some ulcers required major surgery, with all the attendant complications.

Although ulcer patients didn't make out so well under the standard treatment, the medical community did just fine. Millions of patients required the constant service of gastroenterologists and surgeons, while pharmaceutical companies got rich: the antacids Tagamet and Zantac were the first true blockbuster drugs, taking in more than $1 billion a year. By 1994, the global ulcer market was worth more than $8 billion.

In the past, some medical researcher might have suggested that ulcers and other stomach ailments, including cancer, had a different root cause—perhaps even bacterial. But the medical establishment was quick to point out the glaring flaw in this theory: How could bacteria possibly survive in the acidic cauldron of the stomach?

And so the ulcer-treatment juggernaut rolled on. There wasn't much of an incentive to find a cure—not, at least, by the people whose careers depended on the prevailing ulcer treatment.

Fortunately the world is more diverse than that. In 1981, a young Australian medical resident named Barry Marshall was on the hunt for a research project. He had just taken up a rotation in the gastroenterology unit at Royal Perth Hospital, where a senior pathologist had stumbled onto a mystery. As Marshall later described it: "We've got 20 patients with bacteria in their stomach, where you shouldn't have bacteria living because there's too much acid." The senior doctor, Robin Warren, was looking for a young researcher to help "find out what's wrong with these people."

The squiggly bacteria resembled a species called *Campylobacter,* which can cause infection in people who spend time with chickens. Were these human bacteria indeed *Campylobacter*? What kind of diseases might they lead to? And why were they so concentrated among patients with gastric trouble?

Barry Marshall, as it turns out, was already familiar with *Campylobacter,* for his father had worked as a refrigeration engineer in a chicken-packing plant. Marshall's mother, meanwhile, was a nurse. "We used to have a lot of arguments about what was really true in medicine," he told an interviewer, the esteemed medical journalist Norman Swan. "She would 'know' things because they were folklore, and I would say, 'That's old-fashioned. There's no basis for it in fact.' 'Yes, but people have been doing it for hundreds of years, Barry.'"

Marshall was excited by the mystery he inherited. Using samples from Dr. Warren's patients, he tried to culture the squiggly bacteria in the lab. For months, he failed. But after an accident—the culture was left in the incubator three days longer than intended—it finally grew. It wasn't *Campylobacter;* it was a previously undiscovered bacteria, henceforth known as *Helicobacter pylori.*

"We cultured it from lots of people after that," Marshall

recalls. "Then we could say, 'We know which antibiotic kills these bacteria.' We figured out how they could live in the stomach, and we could play around with it in the test tube, do all kinds of useful experiments. . . . We were not looking for the cause of ulcers. We wanted to find out what these bacteria were, and we thought it would be fun to get a nice little publication."

Marshall and Warren continued to look for this bacteria in patients who came to see them with stomach trouble. The doctors soon made a startling discovery: among 13 patients with ulcers, all 13 also had the squiggly bacteria! Was it possible that *H. pylori,* rather than merely showing up in these patients, was actually *causing* the ulcers?

Back in the lab, Marshall tried infecting some rats and pigs with *H. pylori* to see if they developed ulcers. They didn't. "So I said, 'I have to test it out on a human.'"

The human, Marshall decided, would be himself. He also decided not to tell anyone, even his wife or Robin Warren. First he had a biopsy taken of his stomach to make sure he didn't already have *H. pylori.* All clear. Then he swallowed a batch of the bacteria that he had cultured from a patient. In Marshall's mind, there were two likely possibilities:

1. He would develop an ulcer. "And then, hallelujah, it'd be proven."

2. He wouldn't develop an ulcer. "If nothing happened, my two years of research to that point would have been wasted."

Barry Marshall was probably the only person in human history rooting for himself to get an ulcer. If he did, he figured it would take a few years for symptoms to arise.

But just five days after he gulped down the *H. pylori,* Marshall began having vomiting attacks. Hallelujah! After ten days, he had another biopsy taken of his stomach, "and the bacteria were everywhere." Marshall already had gastritis and was apparently well on his way to getting an ulcer. He took an antibiotic to help wipe it out. His and Warren's investigation had proved that *H. pylori* was the true cause of ulcers—and, as further investigation would show, of stomach cancer as well. It was an astonishing breakthrough.

Granted, there was much testing to come—and an enormous pushback from the medical community. Marshall was variously ridiculed, pilloried, and ignored. *Are we to seriously believe that some loopy Australian found the cause of ulcers by swallowing a batch of some bacteria that he says he discovered himself?* No $8 billion industry is ever happy when its reason for being is under attack. Talk about gastric upset! An ulcer, rather than requiring a lifetime of doctor's visits and Zantac and perhaps surgery, could now be vanquished with a cheap dose of antibiotics.

It took years for the ulcer proof to fully take hold, for conventional wisdom dies hard. Even today, many people still believe that ulcers are caused by stress or spicy foods. Fortunately, doctors now know better. The medical community finally came to acknowledge that while everyone else was simply treating the symptoms of an ulcer, Barry Marshall and Robin Warren had uncovered its root cause. In 2005, they were awarded the Nobel Prize.

The ulcer discovery, stunning as it was, constitutes just one small step in a revolution that is only beginning to unfold, a revolution aimed toward finding the root cause of illness rather than simply swatting away symptoms.

H. pylori, it turns out, isn't some lone-wolf bacterial terrorist that managed to slip past security and invade the stomach. In recent years, enterprising scientists—aided by newly powerful computers that facilitate DNA sequencing—have learned that the human gut is home to thousands of species of microbes. Some are good, some are bad, others are *situationally* good or bad, and many have yet to reveal their nature.

Just how many microbes do each of us host? By one estimate, the human body contains ten times as many microbial cells as human cells, which puts the number easily in the trillions and perhaps in the quadrillions. This "microbial cloud," as the biologist Jonathan Eisen calls it, is so vast that some scientists consider it the largest organ in the human body. And within it may lie the root of much human health . . . or illness.

In labs all over the world, researchers have begun to explore whether the ingredients in this sprawling microbial stew—much of which is hereditary—may be responsible for diseases like cancer and multiple sclerosis and diabetes, even obesity and mental illness. Does it seem absurd to think that a given ailment that has haunted humankind for millennia may be caused by the malfunction of a micro-organism that has been merrily swimming through our intestines the whole time?

Perhaps—just as it seemed absurd to all those ulcer doctors and pharmaceutical executives that Barry Marshall knew what he was talking about.

To be sure, these are early days in microbial exploration. The gut is still a frontier—think of the ocean floor or the surface of Mars. But already the research is paying off. A handful of doctors have successfully treated patients suffering from intestinal maladies by giving them a transfusion of healthy gut bacteria.

Where do those healthy bacteria come from, and how are they sluiced into the sick person's gut? Before going further, let us offer two notes of caution:

1. If you happen to be eating as you read this, you may wish to take a break.

2. If you are reading this book many years after it was written (assuming there are still people, and they still read books), the method described below may seem barbarically primitive. In fact we hope that is the case, for it would mean the treatment has proven valuable but that delivery methods have improved.

Okay, so a sick person needs a transfusion of healthy gut bacteria. What is a viable source?

Doctors like Thomas Borody, an Australian gastroenterologist who drew inspiration from Barry Marshall's ulcer research, have identified one answer: human feces. Yes, it appears that the microbe-rich excrement of a healthy person may be just the medicine for a patient whose own gut bacteria are infected, damaged, or incomplete. Fecal matter is obtained from a "donor" and blended into a saline mixture that, according to one Dutch gastroenterologist, looks like chocolate milk. The mixture is then transfused, often via an enema, into the gut of the patient. In recent years, doctors have found fecal transplants to be effective in wiping out intestinal infections that antibiotics could not. In one small study, Borody claims to have used fecal transplants to effectively cure people who were suffering from ulcerative colitis—which, he says, was "previously an incurable disease."

But Borody has been going beyond mere intestinal ailments. He claims to have successfully used fecal transplants to treat patients with multiple sclerosis and Parkinson's disease. Indeed, while Borody is careful to say that much more research is needed, the list of ailments that may have a root cause living in the human gut is nearly endless.

To Borody and a small band of like-minded brethren who believe in the power of poop, we are standing at the threshold of a new era in medicine. Borody sees the benefits of fecal therapy as "equivalent to the discovery of antibiotics." But first, there is much skepticism to overcome.

"Well, the feedback is very much like Barry Marshall's,"

says Borody. "I was initially ostracized. Even now my colleagues avoid talking about this or meeting me at conferences. Although this is changing. I've just had a nice string of invitations to speak at national and international conferences about fecal transplantation. But the aversion is always there. It'd be much nicer if we could come up with a non-fecal-sounding therapy."

Indeed. One can imagine many patients being turned off by the words *fecal transplant* or, as researchers call it in their academic papers, "fecal microbiota transplantation." The slang used by some doctors ("shit swap") is no better. But Borody, after years of performing this procedure, believes he has finally come up with a less disturbing name.

"Yes," he says, "we call it a 'trans*poo*sion.'"

CHAPTER 5

Think Like a Child

At this point you may be asking yourself: *Seriously?* The power of *poop*? A guy who swallows a beaker full of dangerous bacteria—and, before that, a guy who swallows a year's supply of hot dogs in 12 minutes? Could things possibly get any more childish around here? Is "thinking like a Freak" just code for "thinking like a child"?

Well, not entirely. But when it comes to generating ideas and asking questions, it can be really fruitful to have the mentality of an eight-year-old.

Consider the kind of questions that kids ask. Sure, they may be silly or simplistic or out of bounds. But kids are also relentlessly curious and relatively unbiased. Because they know so little, they don't carry around the preconceptions that often stop people from seeing things as they are. When it comes to solving problems, this is a big advantage. Preconceptions lead us to rule out a huge set of possible solutions simply because they seem unlikely or repugnant; because they don't pass the smell test or have never been tried; because they don't seem sophisticated enough.* But remember, it was a child who finally pointed out that the Emperor's new clothes were in fact no clothes at all.

Kids are not afraid to share their wildest ideas. As long as you can tell the difference between a good idea and a bad one, generating a boatload of ideas, even outlandish ones, can only be a good thing. When it comes to generating ideas, the economic concept of "free disposal" is key. Come up with a terrible idea? No problem—just don't act on it.

Granted, sorting bad ideas from good isn't easy. (One trick that works for us is a cooling-off period. Ideas nearly always seem brilliant when they're hatched, so we never act on a new idea for at least twenty-four hours. It is remarkable how stinky some ideas become after just one day in the sun.) In the end, you may find that only one idea out of twenty is worth pursuing—but you might never have come up with that one unless you were willing to blurt out, childlike, everything that wandered through your brain.

So when it comes to solving problems, channeling your inner child can really pay off. It all starts with thinking small.

---

* It is not even clear that sophistication is such a worthy goal. The word is derived from the Greek *sophists*—"itinerant teachers of philosophy and rhetoric who didn't enjoy a good reputation," one scholar writes; they were "more concerned with winning arguments than arriving at the truth."

. . .

If you meet someone who fancies himself a thought leader or an intellectual, one of the nicest compliments you can pay is to call him a "big thinker." Go ahead, try it, and watch him swell with pride. If he does, we can virtually guarantee you he has no interest in thinking like a Freak.

To think like a Freak means to think small, not big. Why? For starters, every big problem has been thought about endlessly by people much smarter than we are. The fact that it remains a problem means it is too damned hard to be cracked in full. Such problems are intractable, hopelessly complex, brimming with entrenched and misaligned incentives. Sure, there are some truly brilliant people out there and they probably *should* think big. For the rest of us, thinking big means you'll spend a lot of time tilting at windmills.

While thinking small won't win you many points with the typical big thinker, there are at least a few noteworthy advocates of our approach. Sir Isaac Newton, for instance. "To explain all nature is too difficult a task for any one man or even for any one age," he wrote. "Tis much better to do a little with certainty and leave the rest for others that come after than to explain all things by conjecture without making sure of any thing."

Maybe the two of us are biased. Maybe we believe in the power of thinking small only because we are so bad at thinking big. There isn't a single big problem we've come close to solving; we just nibble around the margins. In any case, we've come to the conclusion that it's much better to ask small questions than big ones. Here are a few reasons:

1. Small questions are by their nature less often asked and investigated, and maybe not at all. They are virgin territory for true learning.

2. Since big problems are usually a dense mass of intertwined small problems, you can make more progress by tackling a small piece of the big problem than by flailing away at grand solutions.

3. Any kind of change is hard, but the chances of triggering change on a small problem are much greater than on a big one.

4. Thinking big is, by definition, an exercise in imprecision or even speculation. When you think small, the stakes may be diminished but at least you can be relatively sure you know what you're talking about.

So this all sounds great in theory, but does it really work?

We'd like to think our own track record says yes. While we haven't done much about the worldwide scourge of traffic deaths, we did highlight one category of high-risk behavior that was previously overlooked: drunk walking. Rather than attack the huge problem of corporate embezzlement, we used data from a mom-and-pop bagel-delivery outfit in Washington to learn which factors lead people to steal at work (bad weather and stressful holidays, for instance). While we've done nothing to solve the tragedy of childhood gun deaths, we did single out an even greater childhood killer: backyard swimming accidents.

These modest successes look even more trivial when compared with those of other, like-minded small thinkers. Trillions of dollars have been spent on worldwide education reforms, usually focused on overhauling the system in some way—smaller classrooms, better curricula, more testing, and so on. But as we noted earlier, the raw material in the education system—the students themselves—are often overlooked. Might there be some small, simple, cheap intervention that could help millions of students?

One in four children, it turns out, has subpar eyesight, while a whopping 60 percent of "problem learners" have trouble seeing. If you can't see well, you won't read well, and that makes school extra hard. And yet even in a rich country like the United States, vision screening is often lax and there hasn't been much research on the relationship between poor vision and school performance.

Three economists—Paul Glewwe, Albert Park, and Meng Zhao—happened upon this problem in China. They decided to do some hands-on research in Gansu, a poor and remote province. Out of the roughly 2,500 fourth-, fifth-, and sixth-graders there who needed eyeglasses, only 59 wore them. So the economists ran an experiment. They offered free eyeglasses to half the students and let the other half carry on as before. The cost, about $15 per pair of glasses, was covered by a World Bank research grant.

How did the newly bespectacled students do? After wearing glasses for a year, their test scores showed they'd learned 25 to 50 percent more than their uncorrected peers. Thanks to a $15 pair of glasses!

We're not saying that giving glasses to the schoolkids who need them will fix every education problem, not by a long shot. But when you are fixated on thinking big, this is exactly the kind of small-bore solution you can easily miss.*

Here's another cardinal rule of thinking like a child: don't be afraid of the obvious.

The two of us are sometimes invited to meet with a company or an institution that wants outside help with some kind of problem. Walking in, we usually know next to nothing about how their business works. In most instances in which we wind up being helpful, it is the result of an idea that arose in the first few hours—when, starting from com-

---

* Interestingly, about 30 percent of the Chinese kids who were offered free glasses didn't want them. Some feared that wearing glasses at a young age would ultimately weaken their eyes. Another big fear was being teased. Happily, the "four-eyes" stigma has been reversed elsewhere, especially in the United States, where pop stars and top athletes wear non-prescription glasses as a pure style accessory. By some estimates, a few million Americans routinely wear such "planos"—eyeglasses with plain lenses.

plete ignorance, we asked a question that an insider would never deign to ask. Just as many people are unwilling to say "I don't know," nor do they want to appear unsophisticated by asking a simple question or making an observation that was hidden in plain sight.

The idea for the abortion-crime study we cited earlier arose from the simple observation of a simple set of numbers published in the *Statistical Abstract of the United States* (the kind of book economists leaf through for grins).

What do the numbers say? Nothing more than this: within ten years, the United States went from very few abortions to roughly 1.6 million a year, largely because of *Roe v. Wade,* the Supreme Court decision that made abortion legal in all fifty states.

The average smart person, seeing this spike, might immediately jump to its moral or political ramifications. If, however, you are still in touch with your inner child, your first thought might be: *Wow, 1.6 million of anything is a lot. So . . . that must have affected something!*

If you are willing to confront the obvious, you will end up asking a lot of questions that others don't. *Why does that fourth-grader seem plenty smart in conversation but can't answer a single question when it's written on the blackboard? Sure, driving drunk is dangerous, but what about drunk walking? If an ulcer is caused by stress and spicy foods, why do some people with low stress and bland diets still get ulcers?*

As Albert Einstein liked to say, everything should be

made as simple as possible, but not simpler. This is a beautiful way to address the frictions that bedevil modern society: as grateful as we are for the complex processes that have produced so much technology and progress, we are also dizzied by their sprawl. It is easy to get seduced by complexity; but there is virtue in simplicity too.

Let's return briefly to Barry Marshall, our bacteria-gulping Aussie hero who cracked the ulcer code. His father, you'll remember, was an engineer—in a chicken-packing plant, on whaling boats, and elsewhere. "We always had acetylene, oxyacetylene, electrical gear, machinery in our garage," he recalls. At one point, the family lived near a scrap-metal yard with a lot of army leftovers. Marshall trawled it with vigor. "You could find old torpedoes, beautiful little motors, ack-ack guns—you would sit there and wind the handles on them."

In medical school, Marshall found that most of his peers came from families in which the parents were executives or lawyers, with the upbringing to match. Most of them, he says, "never had a chance to play around with an electrical device or tubes or pipes and pressure and things like that." Marshall's hands-on skills were in great demand when it came time to jolt a frog with electricity.

This difference carried over to Marshall's view of the human body itself. The history of medicine is of course long and occasionally glorious. But for all its seeming embrace of science, medicine has also relied on strands of theology, poetry, even shamanism. As a result, the body has often been seen as an ethereal vessel animated by some ghostly human spirit. In this view, the body's complexities are vast, and to some degree impenetrable. Marshall, meanwhile, saw the body as more of a machine—a wondrous machine, to be sure—operating on the basic principles of engineering, chemistry, and physics. While plainly more complicated than an old torpedo, the body could nonetheless be taken apart, tinkered with, and, to some extent, put back together.

Nor did Marshall ignore the obvious fact that all his ulcer patients had a tummy full of bacteria. At the time, conventional wisdom held that the stomach environment was too acidic for bacteria to thrive. And yet there they were. "People who had seen them had always washed them off to look at the stomach cells underneath," says Marshall, "and just ignored the bacteria stuck all over the surface."

So he asked a beautifully simple question: *What in the heck are these bacteria doing here?* By so doing, he went on to prove that an ulcer is not a failure of the human spirit. It was more like a blown gasket, easy enough to patch up if you knew how.

You may have noticed a common thread in some of the stories we've told—about solving ulcers, eating hot dogs, and blind-tasting wine: the people involved seem to be having a good time as they learn. Freaks like to have fun. This is another good reason to think like a child.

Kids aren't afraid to like the things they like. They don't

say they want to go to the opera when they'd rather play video games. They don't pretend they're enjoying a meeting when they really want to get up and run around. Kids are in love with their own audacity, mesmerized by the world around them, and unstoppable in their pursuit of fun.

But in one of the strangest wrinkles of human development, these traits magically evaporate in most people by their twenty-first birthday.

There are certain realms in which having fun, or even looking like you're having fun, is practically forbidden. Politics, for one; academia too. And while some firms have lately been spicing things up with gamification, most of the business world remains allergic to fun.

Why do so many frown so sternly at the idea of having fun? Perhaps out of fear that it connotes you aren't serious. But best as we can tell, there is no correlation between appearing to be serious and actually being good at what you do. In fact an argument can be made that the opposite is true.

There has been a recent surge in research into "expert performance," hoping to determine what makes people good at what they do. The single-most compelling finding? Raw talent is overrated: people who achieve excellence—whether at golf or surgery or piano-playing—were often not the most talented at a young age, but became expert by endlessly practicing their skills. Is it possible to endlessly practice something you don't enjoy? Perhaps, although neither one of us is capable of it.

Why is it so important to have fun? Because if you love

your work (or your activism or your family time), then you'll want to do more of it. You'll think about it before you go to sleep and as soon as you wake up; your mind is always in gear. When you're that engaged, you'll run circles around other people even if they are more naturally talented. From what we've seen personally, the best predictor of success among young economists and journalists is whether they absolutely love what they do. If they approach their job like—well, a *job*—they aren't likely to thrive. But if they've somehow convinced themselves that running regressions or interviewing strangers is the funnest thing in the world, you know they have a shot.

Perhaps the arena most in need of a fun injection is public policy. Think about how policymakers generally try to shape society: by cajoling, threatening, or taxing people into behaving better. The implication is that if something is fun—gambling or eating cheeseburgers or treating the presidential election like a horse race—then it must be bad for us. But it doesn't have to be that way. Rather than dismiss the fun impulse, why not co-opt it for the greater good?

Consider this problem: Americans are infamously bad at saving money. The personal savings rate is currently about 4 percent. We all know it's important to put away money for emergencies and education and retirement. So why don't we do it? Because it's a lot more fun to spend money than to lock it up in a bank!

Meanwhile, Americans spend roughly $60 billion a year

on lottery tickets. It's hard to deny that playing the lottery is fun. But a lot of people also treat it like an investment. Nearly 40 percent of low-income adults consider the lottery their best chance to ever acquire a large sum of money. As a result, low earners spend a much bigger share of their income on the lottery than higher earners.

Unfortunately, the lottery is a dreadful investment. It typically pays out only 60 percent of the take, far less than any casino or racetrack would dare offer. So for every 100 lottery dollars you "invest," you can expect to lose 40.

But what if the fun part of playing the lottery could somehow be harnessed to help people save money? That is the idea behind a prize-linked savings (PLS) account. Here's how it works. Rather than spend $100 on lottery tickets, you deposit $100 in a bank account. Let's say the going interest rate is 1 percent. In a PLS account, you agree to surrender a small chunk of that interest, perhaps .25 percent, which then gets pooled with all the other small chunks from fellow PLS depositors. What happens to that pool of money? It is periodically paid out in a lump sum to some randomly chosen winner—just like the lottery!

A PLS account won't deliver multimillion-dollar jackpots, since the payout pool is drawn from interest rather than principal. But here's the real benefit: even if you never win the PLS lottery, your original deposit (and the interest) remain in your bank account. That's why some people call it a "no-lose lottery." PLS programs have helped people all over the world save money while at the same time not blowing their hard-earned salary on the lottery. In Michigan, a group of credit unions recently put together a PLS pilot program called "Save to Win." Its first big winner was an eighty-six-year-old woman named Billie June Smith. With a deposit of just $75 into her account, she won a payout of $100,000.

Alas, while a few states are experimenting with similar programs, PLS fever isn't exactly sweeping the nation. Why not? Most states prohibit a PLS because it is a form of lottery, and state law typically allows only one entity to run a lottery: the state itself. (Nice monopoly if you can get it.) Moreover, federal law currently prohibits banks from operating lotteries. You can hardly blame politicians for wanting to keep the exclusive right to that $60 billion in annual lottery revenue. Just keep in mind that as much as you may enjoy playing the lottery, the state is having even more fun—because it always wins.

Consider another big challenge: raising money for charitable projects. The standard approach, which we'll look at more closely in Chapter 6, involves a heart-rending pitch with pictures of suffering children or abused animals. It would seem that the secret to raising money is to make people feel so guilty that they can't hold out any longer. Might there be another way?

People love to gamble. They especially seem to love to gamble online. But as of this writing, most online gambling that involves winning real money is illegal in the United States. And yet Americans love gambling so much that millions of them spend billions of real dollars to play fake slot machines and run virtual farms even though they can't take home a penny. If they happen to win, the money is gobbled up by the companies that run the sites.

So consider the following question. If you are willing to pay $20 for the privilege of playing a fake slot machine or running a virtual farm, do you want the money to end up in the hands of Facebook or Zynga, or would you rather it go to your favorite charity? That is, if the American Cancer Society offered an online game that was just as fun as the one you're already playing, wouldn't you rather the money go there? Wouldn't it be even *more* fun to play the game and make the world a better place at the same time?

That was our hypothesis when we recently helped start a website called SpinForGood.com. It's a social-gaming site where people compete with other players and—if they win—donate the proceeds to their favorite charity. Maybe it's not as fun as keeping the money for yourself, but it's surely better than dropping your winnings into Facebook's or Zynga's big bucket.

Have fun, think small, don't fear the obvious—these are all childlike behaviors that, according to us at least, an adult would do well to hang on to. But how strong is the evidence that this stuff actually works?

Let's consider one situation in which kids are better than adults despite all the years of experience and training that should give adults the edge. Imagine for a moment you are a magician. If your life depended on fooling an audience of adults or an audience of kids, whom would you choose?

The obvious answer would be the kids. Adults, after all, know so much more about how things work. But in reality, kids are harder to fool. "Every magician will tell you the same thing," says Alex Stone, whose book *Fooling Houdini* explores the science of deception. "When you really start to look at magic and how it works—the sort of nuts and bolts of how magic fools us—you start to ask some rather profound questions," he says. "You know, how do we perceive reality? How much of what we perceive is actually real? How much faith can we have in our memories?"

Stone, who holds an advanced physics degree, is himself a lifelong magician. His first gig was his own sixth birthday party. "It didn't go well," he says. "I was heckled. It was terrible. I was unprepared." He got better and has since performed for all types of audiences, including leading scholars in biology, physics, and related fields. "You'd think scientists would be hard to dupe," he says, "but really they're pretty easy."

Many of Stone's tricks include a "double lift," a common sleight in which a magician presents two cards as if they are one. That's how a magician can show you "your" card, then seemingly bury it in the deck and make it reappear back on top. "It's a devastating move," Stone says. "Simple but very convincing." Stone has performed many thousands of double lifts. "I've been burned by an adult layperson—i.e., not a magician—maybe twice in the last ten years. But I've been burned a bunch of times by kids."

Why are kids so much harder to deceive? Stone cites several reasons:

1. A magician is constantly steering and cuing his audience to see what the magician wants them to see. This leaves adults—trained all their lives to follow such cues—especially vulnerable. "Intelligence," says Stone, "doesn't correlate very well with gullibility."

2. Adults are indeed better than kids at "paying attention," or focusing on one task at a time. "This is great for getting stuff done," Stone says, "but it also makes you susceptible to misdirection." Kids' attention, meanwhile, "is more diffuse, which makes them harder to fool."

3. Kids don't buy into dogma. "They're relatively free of assumptions and expectations about how the world works," Stone says, "and magic is all about turning your assumptions and expectations against you. When you're pretending to shuffle a deck, they don't even notice you're shuffling."

4. Kids are genuinely curious. In Stone's experience, an adult may be hell-bent on blowing up a trick in order to upstage the magician. (Such people are called "hammers.") A kid, meanwhile, "is really trying to figure out how the trick works, because

that's what you're doing as a kid—trying to figure out how the world works."

5. In certain ways, kids are simply sharper than adults. "We're getting dumber as we get older, perceptually," says Stone. "We just don't notice as much after 18 or so. So with the double lift, kids may actually be noticing the slight difference in thickness between a single card and two cards stuck together."

6. Kids don't overthink a trick. Adults, meanwhile, seek out non-obvious explanations. "The theories that people come up with!" Stone says. Most tricks, he says, are relatively simple. "But people have the most cockamamie explanations. They'll say, 'You hypnotized me!' Or, 'When you showed me the ace, was it not the ace and you just convinced me it was?' They won't get that you simply forced the card on them."

Stone points to one last advantage that has nothing to do with how kids think, and yet can help them decipher a trick: their height. Stone does mostly close-up magic, "and you really want to see it from head-on or above." Kids, meanwhile, are looking up at the trick from below. "I like this one trick where you make coins jump back and forth. You're back-palming the coin, and if kids are too low they might see it."

So by virtue of being low to the ground, a kid can short-circuit a process that has been laboriously built to be seen from above. Unless you're a magician yourself, you'd never discover this advantage. This is a perfectly Freakish illustration of how, by seeing things from a literally new angle, you can sometimes gain an edge in solving a problem.

That said, we aren't suggesting you should model all your behavior after an eight-year-old. That would almost certainly cause more problems than it solves. But wouldn't it be nice if we all smuggled a few childlike instincts across the border into adulthood? We'd spend more time saying what we mean and asking questions we care about; we might even shed a bit of that most pernicious adult trait: pretense.

Isaac Bashevis Singer, who won the Nobel Prize in Literature, wrote across many genres, including children's books. In an essay called "Why I Write for Children," he explained the appeal. "Children read books, not reviews," he wrote. "They don't give a hoot about the critics." And: "When a book is boring, they yawn openly, without any shame or fear of authority." Best of all—and to the relief of authors everywhere—children "don't expect their beloved writer to redeem humanity."

So please, when you're done reading this book, give it to a kid.

CHAPTER 6

Like Giving Candy to a Baby

Amanda, three years old, had been successfully potty-trained but then backslid. None of the usual enticements—stickers, praise, and the like—could get her back on the toilet.

Her mother was so frustrated that she turned the task over to her father, one of the authors of this book. He was supremely confident. Like most economists, he believed he could solve any problem by setting up the right incentives. The fact that his target was a child made it even simpler.

He got down on his knees and looked Amanda in the eye. "If you go to the toilet," he said, "I'll give you a bag of M&M's."

"Right now?" she asked.

"Right now." He knew that every parenting book frowns on using candy as a bribe, but parenting books are not written by economists.

Amanda trotted off to the toilet, did her business, and raced back to claim her M&M's. Victory! It was hard to say who was prouder, daughter or father.

This scheme worked perfectly for three days—not a single accident. But on the morning of the fourth day, things changed. At 7:02 A.M., Amanda announced: "I have to go to the bathroom!" She did and got her M&M's.

Then, at 7:08 A.M.: "I have to go again." She did, just a quick tinkle, and came for her candy.

At 7:11 A.M.: "I have to go again." Again, Amanda made a minimal deposit in the toilet before claiming her next tranche of M&M's. This went on for longer than any of the interested parties care to remember.

How powerful are the right incentives? Within four days, a little girl went from potty-challenged to having the most finely tuned bladder in history. She simply figured out what it made sense to do given the incentives she faced. There was no fine print, no two-bag limit, no time-interval caveat. There was just a girl, a bag of candy, and a toilet.

If there is one mantra a Freak lives by, it is this: *people respond to incentives.* As utterly obvious as this point may seem, we are amazed at how frequently people forget it, and how often it leads to their undoing. Understanding the incentives of all the players in a given scenario is a fundamental step in solving any problem.

Not that incentives are always so easy to figure out.

Different types of incentives—financial, social, moral, legal, and others—push people's buttons in different directions, in different magnitudes. An incentive that works beautifully in one setting may backfire in another. But if you want to think like a Freak, you must learn to be a master of incentives—the good, the bad, and the ugly.

Let's begin with the most obvious incentive: money. There is probably no quadrant of modern life in which financial incentives do not hold serious sway. Money even shapes the way we are shaped. The average U.S. adult weighs about 25 pounds more today than a few decades ago. If you have a hard time picturing how much extra weight 25 pounds is, take a length of rope and thread it through the handles of three plastic gallon jugs full of milk. Now tie this giant milk necklace around your neck and wear it every day for the rest of your life. That's how much weight the average American has gained. And for every person who hasn't gained a pound, someone else out there is wearing *two* milk-jug necklaces.

Why have we gotten so fat? One reason is that food has gotten so much cheaper over time. In 1971, Americans spent 13.4 percent of their disposable income on food; that number now stands at about 6.5 percent. Not all prices have fallen. Some fresh fruits and vegetables, for instance, cost substantially more today. But other foods—especially the most delicious, fattening, and low-nutrition foods like cookies, potato chips, and soda—have gotten much cheaper. By one measure, a pure high-nutrition diet can cost as much as ten times more than a pure junk-food diet.

So there is little doubt that financial incentives work well, even if the outcome is undesirable. Consider a 2011 traffic accident in the Chinese city of Foshan. A two-year-old girl, walking through an outdoor market, was hit by a van. The driver stopped as the girl's body slid beneath the vehicle. But he didn't get out to help. After a pause, he drove away, running over the body again. The girl later died. The driver eventually turned himself in to the police. A recording that was widely reported to be a phone call with the driver was broadcast on the news. "If she is dead," he explained, "I may pay only about 20,000 yuan"—roughly $3,200. "But if she is injured, it may cost me hundreds of thousands yuan."

There are no Good Samaritan laws in China, and compensatory damages for a long-term injury often run higher than death damages. So while one might wish that the driver had put his moral and civic responsibilities first, the perverse financial incentive may have been too strong to ignore.

And let's consider the most common realm in which financial incentives dictate our behavior: employment. Pretend for a moment (if necessary) that you absolutely love your job—the work itself, your colleagues, the free snacks in the break room. How long would you keep showing up if your boss suddenly cut your salary to $1?

No matter how much fun you have at work—and no matter how often you hear a professional athlete swear he'd play for free—few people are willing to work very hard without getting paid. No CEO in the world, therefore, is so delusional as to expect his employees to show up every day and work hard for *no* money. But there is one gigantic workforce asked to do exactly that. In the United States alone, they number nearly 60 million. Who is this massive, underpaid throng?

Schoolchildren. Sure, some parents pay kids for good grades, but school systems are generally dead-set against financial incentives. Shouldn't kids, the argument goes, be driven by a love of learning rather than cash? Do we really want to turn our children into lab rats who master a maze only to get the cheese? To many educators, the idea of paying for grades is downright disgusting.

But economists aren't so easily disgusted. They are also somewhat pushy—which is how it came to pass that a band of economists recently ran a series of experiments in hundreds of schools across the United States, offering cash prizes to more than 20,000 students. In some cases, the students were paid a few dollars for completing a simple study task. In others, a student could make $20 or $50 by raising their test scores.

How well did the cash-for-grades scheme work? There

was improvement in a few cases—second-graders in Dallas, for instance, read more when they were paid $2 per book— but it was incredibly hard to move the needle on test scores, especially among older students.

Why? The rewards offered to the kids were probably too small. Consider how much effort it takes for a C or D student to start getting A's and B's: come to class regularly and pay attention; do all the homework and study more often; learn to perform well on tests. That's a lot of work for just $50! By comparison, a minimum-wage job pays pretty well.

So what would happen if you paid a student $5,000 for every A? Since no deep-pocketed funder has yet come forth with this kind of money, we don't know for sure—but our guess is that honor rolls across the country would explode with new names.

When it comes to financial incentives, size matters. There are things that people will do for a lot of money that they'd never do for just a few dollars. The most devoted carnivore in the world might well go vegan if the tofu lobby offered him a $10 million stipend. And then there's the tale of an economist on holiday in Las Vegas. He found himself one night in a bar standing beside a gorgeous woman. "Would you be willing to sleep with me for $1 million?" he asked her.

She looked him over. There wasn't much to see—but still, $1 million! She agreed to go back to his room.

"All right then, " he said. "Would you be willing to sleep with me for $100?"

"A hundred dollars!" she shot back. "What do you think I am, a prostitute?"

"We've already established that. Now we're just negotiating the price."

Cash incentives, with all their limitations and wrinkles, are plainly not perfect. But here's the good news: it is often possible to elicit the behavior you want through nonfinancial means. And it's a lot cheaper too.

How to do this?

The key is to learn to climb inside other people's minds to figure out what really matters to them. Theoretically, this shouldn't be so hard. We all have a lot of practice thinking about how *we* respond to incentives. Now it's time to sit on the other side of the table, as in a good marriage, to understand what someone else wants. Yes, it may be money they're after—but just as often they are motivated by wanting to be liked, or not be hated; by wanting to stand out in a crowd, or perhaps not stand out.

The problem is that while some incentives are obvious, many aren't. And simply asking people what they want or need doesn't necessarily work. Let's face it: human beings aren't the most candid animals on the planet. We'll often say one thing and do another—or, more precisely, we'll say what we think other people want to hear and then, in private, do what we want. In economics, these are known as *declared preferences* and *revealed preferences,* and there is often a hefty gap between the two.

When trying to figure out what kind of incentive will work in a given situation, it is crucial to keep your eye on this gap. (Thus the old saying: *Don't listen to what people say; watch what they do.*) Furthermore, it's often the case that when you most desperately want to know someone else's incentives—in a negotiation, for instance—your incentives and theirs are at odds.

How can you determine someone's true incentives? Experiments can help. The psychologist Robert Cialdini, an éminence grise in the study of social influence, has proved this again and again.

In one case, he and some fellow researchers wanted to learn about the incentives that would encourage people to use less electricity at home. They began with a phone survey. The researchers called a diverse set of California residents and asked them: How important are the following factors in your decision to conserve energy?

1. It saves money.
2. It protects the environment.
3. It benefits society.
4. A lot of other people are trying to do it.

Let's see what we have here: a financial incentive (no. 1), a moral incentive (no. 2), a social incentive (no. 3), and what might be called a herd-mentality incentive (no. 4). How would you guess the Californians ranked their reasons for saving energy?

Here are their answers, from most important to least:

1. It protects the environment.
2. It benefits society.
3. It saves money.
4. A lot of other people are trying to do it.

That seems about right, doesn't it? Since conservation is largely seen as a moral and social issue, the moral and social incentives are most important. Next came the financial incentive and, in dead last, the herd mentality. This too seems sensible: who would admit to doing anything—especially an act as important as conservation—just because everyone else is doing it?

The phone survey told Cialdini and his colleagues what people *said* about conservation. But did their actions match their words? To find out, the researchers followed up with a field experiment. Going house to house in one California neighborhood, they hung on each doorknob a placard encouraging residents to save energy in the warm months by using a fan rather than air-conditioning.

But, this being an experiment, the placards were not identical. There were five versions. One had a generic "Energy Conservation" headline, while the others bore headlines that matched up to the four incentives—moral, social, financial, and herd-mentality—from the phone survey:

1. PROTECT THE ENVIRONMENT BY CONSERVING ENERGY

2. DO YOUR PART TO CONSERVE ENERGY FOR FUTURE GENERATIONS

3. SAVE MONEY BY CONSERVING ENERGY

4. JOIN YOUR NEIGHBORS IN CONSERVING ENERGY

The explanatory text on each placard was also different. The "Protect the Environment" placard, for instance, said that "you can prevent the release of up to 262 lbs. of greenhouse gases per month." The "Join Your Neighbors" version merely said that 77 percent of local residents "often use fans instead of air-conditioning."

The researchers, having randomly distributed the different placards, were now able to measure the actual energy use in each home to see which of the placards made the most difference. If the phone survey was to be believed, the "Protect the Environment" and "Do Your Part for Future Generations" placards would work best, while the "Join Your Neighbors" sign would fail. Is that what happened?

Not even close. The clear winner of the four was "Join Your Neighbors." That's right: the herd-mentality incentive beat out the moral, social, and financial incentives. Does this surprise you? If so, maybe it shouldn't. Look around the world and you'll find overwhelming evidence of the herd mentality at work. It influences virtually every aspect of our behavior—what we buy, where we eat, how we vote.

You may not like this idea; none of us wants to admit that we are pack animals. But in a complicated world, running with the herd can make sense. Who has time to think through every decision and all the facts behind it? If everybody around you thinks that conserving energy is a good idea—well, maybe it is. So if you are the person *designing* an incentive scheme, you can use this knowledge to herd people into doing the right thing—even if they're doing it for the wrong reasons.

With any problem, it's important to figure out which incentives will actually work, not just what your moral compass tells you *should* work. The key is to think less about the ideal behavior of imaginary people and more about the actual behavior of real people. Those real people are much more unpredictable.

Consider another Robert Cialdini experiment, this one at Petrified Forest National Park in Arizona. The park had a problem, as it made clear on a warning sign:

YOUR HERITAGE IS BEING VANDALIZED EVERY DAY
BY THEFT LOSSES OF PETRIFIED WOOD OF 14 TONS A YEAR,
MOSTLY A SMALL PIECE AT A TIME.

The sign plainly appealed to the visitors' sense of moral outrage. Cialdini wanted to know if this appeal was effective. So he and some colleagues ran an experiment. They seeded various trails throughout the forest with loose pieces of petrified wood, ready for the stealing. On some trails, they posted a sign warning not to steal; other trails got no sign.

The result? The trails with the warning sign had nearly three times *more* theft than the trails with no signs.

How could this be?

Cialdini concluded that the park's warning sign, designed to send a moral message, perhaps sent a different message as well. Something like: *Wow, the petrified wood is going fast—I'd better get mine now!* Or: *Fourteen tons a year!? Surely it won't matter if I take a few pieces.*

The fact is that moral incentives don't work nearly as well as most people might imagine. "Very often," Cialdini says, "public-service messages are designed to move people in societally desirable directions by telling them how many people are behaving in *un*desirable directions. *So many people are drinking and driving—we have to stop this. Teenage pregnancy is so prevalent in our schools—we have to do something about this. Tax fraud is so rampant that we have to increase the penalties for it.* It's very human but it's a wrong-headed strategy, because the subtext message is that a lot of people just like you are doing this. It legitimizes the undesirable behavior."

Does Cialdini's research depress you? Perhaps it suggests that we humans are incorrigibly felonious, hell-bent on grabbing our fair share and then some; that we are always looking out for ourselves rather than the greater good;

that we are, as the California energy study showed, a big fat pack of liars.

But a Freak wouldn't put it that way. Instead, you'd simply observe that people are complicated creatures, with a nuanced set of private and public incentives, and that our behavior is enormously influenced by circumstances. Once you understand how much psychology is at work when people process incentives, you can use your wiles to create incentive plans that really work—either for your own benefit or, if you prefer, for the greater good.

Brian Mullaney, by the time he hit upon one of the most radical ideas in the history of philanthropy, had already had a couple of other radical ideas.

The first came when he was around thirty years old. He was living the life of "an archetypal yuppie," as he puts it, "a Madison Avenue ad man in an Armani suit and Gucci loafers. I had all the accessories: the gold Rolex, the triple black Porsche, the penthouse apartment."

One of his biggest clients was a plastic-surgery practice on Park Avenue in New York. Their patients were, for the most part, wealthy women looking to get slimmer in one region or more buxom in another. Mullaney often took the subway to visit the client. His ride sometimes coincided with the end of the school day; hundreds of kids would rush onto the train. He noticed that many of them had facial marks: scars, moles, blotches, even misshapen features. Why weren't *they* getting plastic surgery? Mullaney, a big, talkative, ruddy-faced man, had an outlandish idea: he would start up a charity to offer free corrective surgery to public-school kids in New York. He called it Operation Smile.

The project was off to a good start when Mullaney learned there was another charity with the same name. This Operation Smile, based in Virginia, was big time: it sent volunteer medical teams to poor countries around the world to perform plastic surgery on children. Mullaney was wowed. He folded his little Operation Smile into this big one, joined its board, and trailed along on missions to China, Gaza, and Vietnam.

Mullaney soon realized how life-changing a simple surgery could be. When a baby girl in the United States is born with a cleft lip or palate, it is routinely fixed at an early age, leaving just a small scar. But if that same girl is born to poor parents in India, the untreated cleft would likely bloom into a horrible jumble of misshapen lip, gum, and teeth. The girl would be ostracized, with little hope for a good education, job, or marriage. One tiny deformity, so fixable, would lead to "ripples of misery," as Mullaney puts it. What appeared to be purely a humanitarian issue was also an economic one. Indeed, when he pitched Operation Smile to reluctant governments, Mullaney sometimes referred to cleft children as "nonperforming assets" who, with a simple surgery, could be returned to the economic mainstream.

But the demand for cleft repair often outstripped the supply that Operation Smile could offer. Because the organization flew in doctors and surgical equipment from the United States, its time and capacity in a given place were limited. "On every mission, 300 or 400 children would show up begging for treatment," Mullaney recalls, "but we could only help 100 or 150."

In a small village in Vietnam, there was one kid who played soccer every day with the Operation Smile volunteers. They started calling him Soccer Boy. When the mission was over and the Americans were driving away, Mullaney saw Soccer Boy chasing after their bus, his cleft lip still unrepaired. "We were in shock—how could he not have been helped?" As a humanitarian, it hurt; as a businessman, it rankled. "What store," he asks, "turns away 80 percent of its customers?"

Mullaney helped conceive a new business model for Operation Smile. Rather than raise millions of dollars to fly doctors and surgical equipment around the world for limited engagements, what if the money were instead used to equip local doctors to perform cleft surgery year-round? Mullaney calculated that the cost per surgery would drop by at least 75 percent.

The leadership of Operation Smile, however, wasn't as keen about this plan. So Mullaney left to help start a new group, Smile Train. By now he had sold off his ad agency (for eight figures, thank you very much) and devoted himself to fixing the smile of every last Soccer Boy and Girl he could locate. He also wanted to change the face of the nonprofit industry itself, "the most dysfunctional $300 billion industry in the world," as he saw it. Mullaney had come to believe that too many philanthropists engage in what Peter

Buffett, a son of the über-billionaire Warren Buffett, calls "conscience laundering"—doing charity to make themselves feel better rather than fighting to figure out the best ways to alleviate suffering. Mullaney, the archetypal yuppie, had become a data-driven do-gooder.

Smile Train was phenomenally successful. Over the next fifteen years, it helped provide more than 1 million surgeries in nearly 90 countries, all with a worldwide staff of fewer than 100. A documentary film called *Smile Pinki,* which Mullaney helped produce, won an Academy Award. Not coincidentally, Mullaney had turned the organization into a fund-raising juggernaut, taking in nearly $1 billion all told. The skills that had been useful as an ad man were useful as a fund-raiser too—targeting potential donors, honing the Smile Train message, and pitching its mission with just the right blend of pathos and verve. (He also knew how to buy up *New York Times* "remnant" ad space at a fraction of the sticker price.)

Along the way, Brian Mullaney learned a great deal about the incentives that lead people to give money to a charity. This led him to try something so unusual that, as he says, "many people thought we were crazy."

The idea began with a simple question: Why *do* people give money to charity?

This is one of those obvious questions that most smart people might not think to ask. Mullaney became consumed by it. A raft of academic research pointed to two main reasons:

1. People are truly altruistic, driven by a desire to help others.

2. Giving to charity makes them feel better about themselves; economists call this "warm-glow altruism."

Mullaney didn't doubt these two factors. But he thought there was a third factor, which people didn't talk about:

3. Once people are asked to donate, the social pressure is so great that they get bullied into giving, even though they wish they'd never been asked in the first place.

Mullaney knew that number 3 was important to Smile Train's success. That's why their millions of mailings included a photograph of a disfigured child in need of cleft surgery. While no fund-raiser in his right mind would ever publicly admit to manipulating donors with social pressure, everyone knew how strong this incentive was.

But what if, Mullaney thought, instead of downplaying the pressure, Smile Train were to highlight it? That is, what if Smile Train offered potential donors a way to alleviate the social pressure and give money at the same time?

That's how a strategy known as "once-and-done" was born. Here's what Smile Train would tell potential donors: *Make one gift now and we'll never ask for another donation again.*

As far as Mullaney knew, a once-and-done strategy had never been tried before—and with good reason! In fund-raising, acquiring a new donor is difficult and expensive. Almost every charity initially loses money in this phase. But donors, once hooked, tend to give again and again. The secret to fund-raising success is cultivating these repeat givers—so the last thing you'd want to do is set them free as soon as you've hooked them. "Why would you ever agree to *not* harass donors when harassing is the main ingredient for success in direct mail?" Mullaney says.

Smile Train took this harassment seriously. If you made an initial donation, you could expect an average of eighteen mailings a year. Once you gave to Smile Train, you were getting into a long-term relationship whether you liked it or not. But Mullaney suspected there was a whole universe of other people out there with no interest in a long-term relationship—and, indeed, who might be annoyed by Smile Train's stalking. These people, he hypothesized, might be willing to pay Smile Train to *stop* sending them mail. Rather than getting into a long-term relationship, maybe they would consent to a single date with Smile Train as long as Smile Train promised to never ask them out again.

Mullaney tested this idea by launching a direct-mail experiment that included hundreds of thousands of letters with the once-and-done message. Even Mullaney, who never met a piece of conventional wisdom he liked, wasn't sure this was a good idea. Once-and-done could be an unmitigated failure.

How did it work out?

Households that got the once-and-done letter were *twice* as likely to become first-time donors as people who got a regular solicitation letter. By fund-raising standards, this was a colossal gain. These donors also gave slightly more money, an average of $56 versus $50.

So Smile Train quickly raised millions of extra dollars. But were they sacrificing long-term donations for short-term gains? After all, every new donor now had the option to tell Smile Train to kindly get lost forever. The once-and-done mailing contained a reply card that asked a donor to check one of three boxes:

1. *This will be my only gift. Please send me a tax receipt and do not ask for another donation again.*

2. *I would prefer to receive only two communications from The Smile Train each year. Please honor my wishes to limit the amount of mail sent to me.*

3. *Please keep me up-to-date on the progress The Smile Train is making on curing the world of clefts by sending me regular communications.*

You might expect all new donors would tick off box number 1. After all, that was the promise that got them in the door. But only about one-third of them opted out of future mailings! Most donors were happy to let Smile Train keep harassing them—and, as the data would eventually show, they were also happy to keep giving money. The once-and-done operation raised overall donations by an astonishing 46 percent. And because some people *did* opt out of future mailings, Smile Train raised all that money by sending fewer letters, which saved a bundle on expenses.

The only failure of once-and-done was its name: most donors didn't give just once and they weren't in any hurry to be done with Smile Train.

Why did Brian Mullaney's gamble work so well? There are several explanations:

1. *Novelty*. When is the last time a charity—or any kind of company—offered to never bother you again? That alone is enough to get your attention.

2. *Candor*. Have you ever heard a charity acknowledge what a hassle it is to get all those beseeching letters in the mail? In a world of crooked information, it is nice to hear some straight talk.

3. *Control*. Rather than unilaterally dictate the terms of the transaction, Smile Train gave the donor some power. Who doesn't like to control their own destiny?

There is one more factor that made once-and-done successful, a factor so important—subtle and powerful at the same time—that we believe it is the secret ingredient to make any incentive work, or at least work better. The most radical accomplishment of once-and-done is that it *changed the frame of the relationship* between the charity and the donor.

Whenever you interact with another entity, whether it's your best friend or some faceless bureaucracy, the interaction falls into one of a handful of frameworks. There's the financial framework that governs everything we buy, sell, and trade. There's an "us-versus-them" framework that defines war, sports, and, unfortunately, most political activity. The "loved-one" framework covers friends and family (at least when things are going smoothly; otherwise, look out for "us-versus-them"). There's a collaborative framework that shapes how you behave with work colleagues or in your amateur orchestra or pickup soccer team. And then there's the "authority-figure" framework, in which someone gives instructions and someone else is expected to follow them—think of parents, teachers, police and military officers, and a certain kind of boss.

Most of us breeze in and out of these different frameworks every day without needing to think about the boundaries. We've been conditioned to understand that we behave differently in different frameworks, and that incentives work differently too.

Let's say a friend invites you to a dinner party at his house. It's a great, festive evening—who knew your friend was such a paella stud?!—and on the way out you give him a big thank-you and a $100 bill.

Oops.

Now imagine you've taken a date to a nice restaurant. Again, you have a fantastic time. On your way out, you tell the owner how much you enjoyed the meal and give him a big, friendly hug—but don't pay the check.

Double oops.

In the second case, you ignored the obvious rules of the financial framework (and maybe got arrested). In the first, you polluted the loved-ones framework by bringing money into play (and maybe lost a friend).

So you can plainly get into trouble by getting your frames mixed up. But it can also be incredibly productive to nudge a relationship from one framework into another. Whether through subtle cues or concrete incentives, a lot of problems can be solved by shifting the dynamic between parties, whether it's two people or two billion.

In the early 1970s, the relationship between the United States and China was frigid, as it had been for years. China saw the Americans as thoughtless imperialists while the U.S. saw the Chinese as heartless communists—and, worse, a staunch Cold War ally of the Soviet Union. Nearly every encounter between the two countries fell into an us-versus-them framework.

That said, there were all sorts of reasons—political, financial, and otherwise—for China and the U.S. to reach a détente. Indeed, back-channel negotiations were under way. But decades of political friction had produced a stalemate that wouldn't allow for direct talks between the two countries. There was too much pride at stake, too much face to save.

Enter the Ping-Pong teams. On April 6, 1971, a Chinese team showed up in Japan to compete in an international tournament. It was the first Chinese sports team to play outside the country in more than twenty years. But Ping-Pong wasn't their only mission. The team carried from Chairman Mao himself a message "to invite the American team to visit China." And so a week later, the American Ping-Pong team found itself chatting face-to-face with Zhou Enlai, the Chinese premier, at the Great Hall of the People in Beijing.

President Richard Nixon hurriedly sent Henry Kissinger, his secretary of state, on a secret diplomatic mission to Beijing. If the Chinese leadership was willing to receive Ping-Pong ambassadors, why not a real one? Kissinger's visit led to two developments: an invitation for the Chinese Ping-Pong team to visit the United States and, more substantially, Nixon's historic trip to China. It was, as Nixon later called it, "the week that changed the world." Would all this have happened without the Ping-Pong diplomacy that so coyly shifted the us-versus-them framework? Perhaps. But Premier Zhou for one acknowledged just how effective the move was: "Never before in history has a sport been used so effectively as a tool of international diplomacy."

Even when the stakes are not so high as this, changing the framework of a relationship can produce rapture. Consider the following testimonial:

*You guys are just the best. I have sent so many people
to your site. . . . You are really doing something right!!
Don't change a bit! Thank you!!!*

Who is being praised here—a rock band? A sports team?
Or maybe . . . an online shoe store?

In 1999, a company called Zappos started selling shoes
over the web. Later, it added clothing. Like a lot of modern companies built by young entrepreneurs, Zappos was
driven less by pure financial incentives than a desire to
be loved. Customer service, it declared, would be its defining strength. Not just your standard customer service,
but way-over-the-top, call-us-anytime, there's-nothing-we-
won't- do-for-you customer service.

To outsiders, this seemed bizarre. If ever a business were
made for *not* having to coddle customers, online shoe sales
would seem to be it. But Zappos had a different idea.

To the average company, a customer is a human wal-
let from which the company attempts to extract as much
money as possible. Everyone understands this, but no company wants it to be so explicit. That's why companies use
super-friendly logos, slogans, mascots, and endorsers.

Zappos, meanwhile, rather than faking friendli-
ness, seemed to actually want to become friendly with its
customers—at least inasmuch as it would help the company
succeed. Which is why, rather than bury its phone number
deep within the website, Zappos posted its number atop
every page and staffed its call center 24/7. (Some calls, so

long and intimate, resemble "protracted talk therapy," as one observer noted.) Which is why Zappos offered a 365-day return window and free shipping. Which is why, when one customer failed to return a pair of shoes because of a death in the family, Zappos sent her flowers.

To shift the framework like this—from a conventional financial one to a quasi-friendly one—Zappos first needed to shift the framework between the company itself and its workers.

A call-center job isn't typically very desirable, nor does it pay well. (In Las Vegas, where Zappos is based, customer-service representatives made about $11 an hour.) So how could Zappos recruit a better breed of customer rep?

The standard answer would be to pay them more. But Zappos couldn't afford that. Instead, it offered more fun and more power. That's why company meetings are sometimes held in a bar. And why a stroll through the cubicles at Zappos feels like a trip to Mardi Gras, with music, games, and costumes. Customer reps are encouraged to talk to a customer for as long as they want (all without a script, natch); they are authorized to settle problems without calling in a supervisor and can even "fire" a customer who makes trouble.

Just how desirable is a call-center job at Zappos? In a recent year when it hired 250 new employees, the company fielded 25,000 applications—for a job that pays only $11 per hour!

The most impressive result of all this frame-shifting? It

worked: Zappos smoked the competition and became what is thought to be the biggest online shoe store in the world. In 2009, it was bought by Amazon.com for a reported $1.2 billion. Amazon, to its credit, appreciated what made Zappos thrum. In its SEC filing, Amazon noted that it would preserve the Zappos management team and its "customer-obsessed culture."

And let's not forget how Smile Train shifted the relationship between itself and its donors. As much as people might like to think charitable giving is all about the altruism, the old ad salesman Brian Mullaney knew better. He was selling a product (in Smile Train's case, a sad story) and the donor was buying (a happy ending).

The once-and-done campaign changed that. Rather than hound donors with a hard sell, Smile Train changed its message: *Hey, we know it's a hassle to get eighteen letters a year. You think we like having to send out that many? But we're all in this fight together, so why don't you send us a few bucks and we can be done with it?*

Voilà! The financial framework had been recast as a collaborative one, leaving all parties—and most especially the Soccer Boys and Girls of the world—in better shape.

We don't mean to create the impression that any problem can be fixed with a simple shift of the framework or a clever incentive. It can be frightfully hard to come up with incentives that work and continue to work over time. (Remember how easily a three-year-old girl with a taste for M&M's

played her father?) Plenty of incentives fail—and some fail so spectacularly that they produce even more of the bad behavior they were meant to stop.

Mexico City has long suffered from dreadful traffic jams. The pollution is horrendous and it's hard to get anywhere on time. Out of desperation, the government came up with a rationing plan. Drivers would have to leave their cars home one workday each week, with the particular day determined by the car's license-plate number. The hope was that fewer cars would clog the roads, more people would use public transportation, and pollution would fall.

How did the plan work out?

The rationing led to *more* cars in circulation, no increase in the use of public transportation, and no improvement in air quality. Why? In order to skirt the license-plate ban, a lot of people went out and bought a second car—many of which were older, cheaper gas guzzlers.

In another case, the United Nations set up an incentive plan to compensate manufacturers for curtailing the pollutants they released into the atmosphere. The payments, in the form of carbon credits that could be sold on the open market, were indexed to the environmental harm of each pollutant.

For every ton of carbon dioxide a factory eliminated, it would receive one credit. Other pollutants were far more remunerative: methane (21 credits), nitrous oxide (310), and, near the top of the list, something called hydrofluorocarbon-23, or HFC-23. It is a "super" greenhouse gas that is a by-product in the manufacture of HCFC-22, a common refrigerant that is itself plenty bad for the environment.

The UN was hoping that factories would switch to a greener refrigerant than HCFC-22. One way to incentivize them, it reasoned, was to reward the factories handsomely for destroying their stock of its waste gas, HFC-23. So the UN offered a whopping bounty of 11,700 carbon credits for every ton of HFC-23 that was destroyed rather than released into the atmosphere.

Can you guess what happened next?

Factories around the world, especially in China and India, began to churn out extra HCFC-22 in order to generate extra HFC-23 so they could rake in the cash. As an official with the Environmental Investigation Agency (EIA) put it: "The evidence is overwhelming that manufacturers are creating excess HFC-23 simply to destroy it and earn carbon credits." The average factory earned *more than $20 million* a year by selling carbon credits for HFC-23.

Angry and embarrassed, the UN changed the rules of the program to curb the abuse; several carbon markets banned the HFC-23 credits, making it harder for the factories to find buyers. So what will happen to all those extra tons of harmful HFC-23 that suddenly lost its value? The EIA warns that China and India may well "release vast amounts of . . . HFC-23 into the atmosphere, causing global greenhouse gas emissions to skyrocket."

Which means the UN wound up paying polluters millions upon millions of dollars to . . . create additional pollution.

Backfiring bounties are, sadly, not as rare as one might hope. This phenomenon is sometimes called "the cobra effect." As the story goes, a British overlord in colonial India thought there were far too many cobras in Delhi. So he offered a cash bounty for every cobra skin. The incentive worked well—so well, in fact, that it gave rise to a new industry: cobra farming. Indians began to breed, raise, and slaughter the snakes to take advantage of the bounty. Eventually the bounty was rescinded—whereupon the cobra farmers did the logical thing and set their snakes free, as toxic and unwanted as today's HFC-23.

And yet, if you look around the world, you will see that cash bounties are still routinely offered to get rid of pests. Most recently, we've heard of this happening with feral pigs in Georgia and rats in South Africa. And, just as routinely, an army of people rise up to game the system. As Mark Twain once wrote: "[T]he best way to increase wolves in America, rabbits in Australia, and snakes in India is to pay a bounty on their scalps. Then every patriot goes to raising them."

Why do some incentives, even those created by smart and well-intentioned people, backfire so badly? We can think of at least three reasons:

1. No individual or government will ever be as smart as all the people out there scheming to beat an incentive plan.

2. It's easy to envision how you'd change the behavior of people who think just like you do, but the people whose behavior you're trying to change often *don't* think like you—and, therefore, don't respond as you might expect.

3. There is a tendency to assume that the way people behave today is how they'll always behave. But the very nature of an incentive suggests that when a rule changes, behavior does too—although not necessarily, as we've seen, in the expected direction.

We should also note the obvious point that no one likes to feel manipulated. Too many incentive schemes are thinly disguised grabs for leverage or money, so it shouldn't be surprising that some people push back. Thinking like a Freak may sometimes sound like an exercise in using clever means to get exactly what you want, and there's nothing wrong with that. But if there is one thing we've learned from a lifetime of designing and analyzing incentives, the best way to get what you want is to treat other people with decency. Decency can push almost any interaction into the cooperative frame. It is most powerful when least expected, like when things have gone wrong. Some of the most loyal customers any company has are the ones who had a big problem but got treated incredibly well as it was being resolved.

So while designing the right incentive scheme certainly isn't easy, here's a simple set of rules that usually point us in the right direction:

1. Figure out what people *really* care about, not what they say they care about.

2. Incentivize them on the dimensions that are valuable to them but cheap for you to provide.

3. Pay attention to how people respond; if their response surprises or frustrates you, learn from it and try something different.

4. Whenever possible, create incentives that switch the frame from adversarial to cooperative.

5. Never, ever think that people will do something just because it is the "right" thing to do.

6. Know that some people will do everything they can to game the system, finding ways to win that you never could have imagined. If only to keep yourself sane, try to applaud their ingenuity rather than curse their greed.

That's Incentives 101. Pretty simple, right? Now you're ready for an advanced degree in incentive scheming. We begin the journey with a question that, to our knowledge, has never been asked in the history of humankind.

CHAPTER 7

What Do King Solomon and David Lee Roth Have in Common?

King Solomon built the First Temple in Jerusalem and was known throughout the land for his wisdom.

David Lee Roth fronted the rock band Van Halen and was known throughout the land for his prima-donna excess.

What could these two men conceivably have in common? Here are a few possibilities:

1. Both of them were Jewish.
2. They both got a lot of girls.
3. They both wrote the lyrics to a number-one pop song.
4. They both dabbled in game theory.

As it happens, all four of these statements are true. Some confirmatory facts:

1. David Lee Roth was born into a Jewish family in Bloomington, Indiana, in 1954; his father, Nathan, was an ophthalmologist. (It was while preparing for his bar mitzvah that David learned to sing.) King Solomon was born into a Jewish family in Jerusalem, circa 1000 BCE; his father, David, had also been king.

2. David Lee Roth "slept with every pretty girl with two legs in her pants," he once said. "I even slept with an amputee." King Solomon "loved many foreign women," according to the Bible, including "seven hundred wives, princesses, and three hundred concubines."

3. David Lee Roth wrote the lyrics for most of Van Halen's songs, including its sole number-one hit, "Jump." King Solomon is thought to have authored some or all of the biblical books *Proverbs*, *Song of Songs*, and *Ecclesiastes*. The folk singer Pete Seeger used several verses from *Ecclesiastes* as lyrics to his song "Turn! Turn! Turn!"—which, when recorded by the Byrds in 1965, became a number-one hit.*

4. One of the most famous stories about each man involves a clever piece of strategic thinking that anyone who wishes to think like a Freak would do well to mimic.

---

* Another weird Solomon-Roth commonality: the titles of both of their number-one songs include only a single imperative verb.

Solomon, a young man when he inherited the throne, was eager to prove his judgment was sound. He was soon given a chance to do that when two women, prostitutes by trade, came to him with a dilemma. The women lived in the same house and, within the space of a few days, had each given birth to a baby boy. The first woman told the king that the second woman's baby died, and that the second woman "arose at midnight, and took my son from beside me . . . and laid the dead child in my bosom." The second woman disputed the story: "Nay; but the living is my son, and the dead is thy son."

One of the women was plainly lying, but which one? How was King Solomon supposed to tell who was the mother of the living child?

"Fetch me a sword," he said. "Divide the living child in two, and give half to the one, and half to the other."

The first woman begged the king to not hurt the baby, and instead give it to the second woman.

The second woman, however, embraced the king's solution: "It shall be neither mine nor thine," she said. "Divide it."

King Solomon promptly ruled in favor of the first woman. "Give her the living child," he said. "She is the mother thereof." The Bible tells us that "all Israel heard of the judgment" and they "saw that the wisdom of God was in him, to do justice."

How did Solomon know the true mother?

He reasoned that a woman cruel enough to go along

with his baby-carving plan was cruel enough to steal another's child. And, further, that the real mother would rather give up her child than see it die. King Solomon had set a trap that encouraged the guilty and the innocent to sort themselves out.*

As clever as that was, David Lee Roth may have been a bit cleverer. By the early 1980s, Van Halen had become one of the biggest rock-and-roll bands in history. They were known to party particularly hard while on tour. "[N]o matter where Van Halen alights," *Rolling Stone* reported, "a boisterous, full-blown saturnalia is bound to follow."

The band's touring contract carried a fifty-three-page rider that laid out technical and security specs as well as food and beverage requirements. On even calendar days, the band was to be served roast beef, fried chicken, or lasagna, with sides of Brussels sprouts, broccoli, or spinach. Odd days meant steak or Chinese food with green beans, peas, or carrots. Under no circumstances was dinner to be served on plastic or paper plates, or with plastic flatware.

On page 40 of the exhaustive Van Halen rider was the "Munchies" section. It demanded potato chips, nuts, pret-

---

* As careful readers will recall, the competitive-eating champion Takeru Kobayashi tore his hot dogs in half in order to eat them faster, a move that came to be known as the Solomon Method. An even more careful reader will note this is a misnomer, for while King Solomon threatened to cut the disputed baby in half, he didn't actually do it.

zels, and "M&M's (<u>WARNING: ABSOLUTELY NO BROWN ONES</u>)."*

What was up with that? The nut and chip requests weren't nearly so nitpicky. Nor the dinner menu. So why the hang-up with brown M&M's? Had someone in the band had a bad experience with them? Did Van Halen have a sadistic streak and take pleasure in making some poor caterer hand-sort the M&M's?

When the M&M clause was leaked to the press, it was seen as a classic case of rock-star excess, of the band "being abusive of others simply because we could," Roth said years later. But, he explained, "the reality is quite different."

Van Halen's live show was an extravaganza, with a colossal stage set, booming audio, and spectacular lighting effects. All this equipment required a great deal of structural support, electrical power, and the like. But many of the arenas they played were outdated. "[T]hey didn't have even the doorways or the loading docks to accommodate a super-forward-thinking, gigantor, epic-sized Van Halen production," Roth recalled.

Thus the need for a fifty-three-page rider. "Most rock-and-roll bands had a contract rider that was like a pamphlet," Roth says. "We had one that was like the Chinese

---

* The fact that this chapter and the previous one include stories about non-traditional uses of M&M's is entirely coincidental. We have received no product-placement or endorsement money from Mars, the maker of M&M's—although in retrospect we are sort of embarrassed that we didn't.

phone book." It gave point-by-point instructions to ensure that the promoter at each arena provided enough physical space, load-bearing capacity, and electrical power. Van Halen wanted to make sure no one got killed by a collapsing stage or a short-circuiting light tower.

But every time the band pulled into a new city, how could they be sure the local promoter had read the rider and followed all the safety procedures?

Cue the brown M&M's. When Roth arrived at the arena, he'd immediately go backstage to check out the bowl of M&M's. If he saw brown ones, he knew the promoter hadn't read the rider carefully—and that "we had to do a serious line check" to make sure the important equipment had been properly set up.

He also made sure to trash the dressing room if there *were* brown M&M's. This would be construed as nothing more than rock-star folly, thereby keeping his trap safe from detection. But we suspect he enjoyed it all the same.

And so it was that David Lee Roth and King Solomon both engaged in a fruitful bit of game theory—which, narrowly defined, is the art of beating your opponent by anticipating his next move.

There was a time when economists thought that game theory would take over the world, helping to shape or predict all sorts of important outcomes. Alas, it proved to be not nearly as useful or interesting as promised. In most cases, the world is too complicated for game theory to work its supposed magic. But again, thinking like a Freak means thinking simply—and as King Solomon and David Lee Roth showed, a simple version of game theory can work wonders.

As disparate as their settings were, the two men faced a similar problem: a need to sift the guilty from the innocent when no one was stepping forward to profess their guilt. In economist-speak, there was a "pooling equilibrium"—the two mothers in Solomon's case, and all the tour promoters in Van Halen's case—that needed to be broken down into a "separating equilibrium."

A person who is lying or cheating will often respond to an incentive differently than an honest person. How can this fact be exploited to ferret out the bad guys? Doing so requires an understanding of how incentives work in general (which you gained in the last chapter) and how different actors may respond differently to a given incentive (as we'll discuss in this one). Certain tools in the Freak arsenal may come in handy only once or twice in your lifetime. This is one such tool. But it has power and a certain elegance, for it can entice a guilty party to unwittingly reveal his guilt through his own behavior.

What is this trick called? We have scoured history books and other texts to find a proper name for it, but came up empty. So let's make up something. In honor of King Solomon, we'll treat this phenomenon as if it were a lost proverb: Teach Your Garden to Weed Itself.

• • •

Imagine you've been accused of a crime. The police say you stole something or beat up someone or perhaps drunkenly drove your vehicle through a park and mowed down everyone in sight.

But the evidence is murky. The judge assigned to your case does her best to figure out what happened, but she can't be sure. So she comes up with a creative solution. She decrees that you will plunge your arm into a cauldron of boiling water. If you come away unhurt, you will be declared innocent and set free; but if your arm is disfigured, you will be convicted and sent to prison.

This is precisely what happened in Europe for hundreds of years during the Middle Ages. If the court couldn't satisfactorily determine whether a defendant was guilty, it turned the case over to a Catholic priest who would administer an "ordeal" that used boiling water or a smoking-hot iron bar. The idea was that God knew the truth and would miraculously deliver from harm any suspect who had been wrongly accused.

As a means of establishing guilt, how would you characterize the medieval ordeal?

1. Barbaric
2. Nonsensical
3. Surprisingly effective

Before you answer, let's think about the incentives at play here. Picture a shepherd living in the north of England some one thousand years ago. We'll call him Adam. He has a next-door neighbor, Ralf, who is also a shepherd. The two of them don't get along. Adam suspects that Ralf once stole a few of his sheep. Ralf spreads word that Adam packs his wool bales with stones to drive up their weight at market. The two men regularly quarrel over rights to a communal grazing meadow.

One morning, Ralf's entire flock of sheep turns up dead, apparently poisoned. He promptly accuses Adam. While Adam may indeed have an incentive to kill Ralf's flock—less wool from Ralf means a higher price for Adam—there are certainly other possibilities. Maybe the sheep died of disease or a natural poison. Maybe they were poisoned by a third rival. Or perhaps Ralf poisoned the sheep *himself* in order to get Adam sent to prison or fined.

Evidence is collected and brought before the court, but it is hardly conclusive. Ralf claims he spotted Adam lurking near his flock the night before the incident, but given the rivals' acrimony, the judge wonders if Ralf is lying.

Imagine now that you are the judge: How are you supposed to determine whether Adam is guilty? And imagine further that instead of one such case, there are 50 Adams before the court. In each instance, the evidence is too weak to convict, but you also don't want to set a criminal free. How can the innocent be weeded from the guilty?

By letting the garden weed itself.

The judge gives each Adam two choices. He can either plead guilty or submit to a trial by ordeal, putting his fate in God's hands. From our modern perspective, it's hard to imagine an ordeal as an effective way to separate the guilty from the innocent—but was it?

Let's take a look at the data. The economist Peter Leeson, whose research has covered topics like Gypsy law and pirate economics, did just that. One set of church records from thirteenth-century Hungary included 308 cases that entered the trial-by-ordeal phase. Of these, 100 were aborted before producing a final result. That left 208 cases in which the defendant was summoned by a priest to the church, climbed the altar, and—after his fellow congregants were ushered in to observe from a distance—was forced to grab hold of a red-hot iron bar.

How many of those 208 people do you think were badly burned? All 208? Don't forget, we're talking about red-hot iron here. Maybe 207 or 206?

The actual number is 78. Which means that the remaining 130—nearly two-thirds of the defendants who underwent the ordeal—were miraculously unharmed and thereby exonerated.

Unless these 130 miracles in fact *were* miracles, how can they be explained?

Peter Leeson thinks he knows the answer: "priestly rigging." That is, a priest somehow tinkered with the setup to make the ordeal look legitimate while ensuring that the defendant wouldn't be disfigured. This wouldn't have been difficult, since the priest had ultimate control over the entire situation. Maybe he swapped out the red-hot bar of iron for a cooler one. Or, when using the boiling-water ordeal, maybe he dumped a pail of cold water into the cauldron before the congregants entered the church.

Why would a priest do this? Was he simply exercising a bit of human mercy? Did he perhaps accept bribes from certain defendants?

Leeson sees a different explanation. Let's think back to those 50 Adams on which the court is undecided. We'll assume that some are guilty and some innocent. As noted earlier, a guilty person and an innocent one will often respond to the same incentive in different ways. What are the guilty Adams and the innocent Adams thinking in this case?

A guilty Adam is probably thinking something like this: *God knows I am guilty. If, therefore, I undergo the ordeal, I will be horribly scalded. Not only will I then be imprisoned or fined, but I'll spend the rest of my life in pain. So perhaps I should go ahead and confess my guilt in order to avoid the ordeal.*

And what would an innocent Adam think? *God knows I am innocent. I will therefore undergo the ordeal, since God would never allow this fiery curse to harm me.*

So the belief that God would intervene in their trial by ordeal, Leeson writes, "created a separating equilibrium in which only innocent defendants were willing to undergo ordeals." This helps explain why 100 of the 308 ordeals were aborted: the defendants in these cases settled with the plaintiff—presumably, at least in many instances, because the defendant was guilty and figured he'd be better off accepting his punishment without the additional penalty of being burned.

And what about our shepherd Adam? Let's say for the sake of argument that he did *not* poison Ralf's flock and was framed by Ralf. What would Adam's fate be? By the time he stood in the church before the bubbling cauldron, praying for mercy, the priest would likely have reckoned that Adam was innocent. So he'd rig the ordeal accordingly.

Let's not forget that 78 defendants in this data set *were* scalded and then fined or sent to prison. What happened in those cases?

Our best explanation is that either (1) the priests believed these defendants really were guilty; or (2) the priests had to at least keep up appearances that a trial by ordeal really worked, or else the threat would lose its power to sort the innocent from the guilty—and so these folks were sacrificed.

We should also note that the threat would lose its power if the defendants didn't believe in an all-powerful, all-knowing God who punished the guilty and pardoned the innocent. But history suggests that most people at the time did indeed believe in an all-powerful, justice-seeking God.

Which leads us to the most bizarre twist in this bizarre story: if medieval priests did manipulate the ordeals, that might make them the only parties who thought an all-knowing God *didn't* exist—or if he did, that he had enough faith in his priestly deputies to see their tampering as part of a divine quest for justice.

. . .

You too can play God once in a while if you learn to set up a self-weeding garden.

Let's say you work for a company that hires hundreds of new employees each year. Hiring takes a lot of time and money, especially in industries in which workers come and go. In the retail trade, for instance, employee turnover is roughly 50 percent annually; among fast-food workers, the rate can approach 100 percent.

So it isn't surprising that employers have worked hard to streamline the application process. Job seekers can now fill out online applications in twenty minutes from the comfort of their homes. Great news, right?

Maybe not. Such an easy application process may attract people with only minimal interest in the job, who look great on paper but aren't likely to stick around long if hired.

So what if employers, rather than making the application process ever easier, made it unnecessarily onerous—with, say, a 60- or 90-minute application that weeds out the dilettantes?

We've pitched this idea to a number of companies, and have gotten exactly zero takers. Why? "If we make the application process longer," they say, "we'll get fewer applicants." That, of course, is exactly the point: you'd immediately get rid of the applicants who are more likely to not show up on time or quit after a few weeks.

Colleges and universities, meanwhile, have no such

qualms about torturing their applicants. Think about how much work a high-school student must do to even be considered for a spot at a decent college. The difference in college and job applications is especially striking when you consider that a job applicant will be getting paid upon acceptance while a college applicant will be paying for the privilege to attend.

But this does help explain why a college degree remains so valuable. (In the United States, a worker with a four-year degree earns about 75 percent more than someone with only a high-school degree.) What sort of signal does a college diploma send to a potential employer? That its holder is willing and able to complete all sorts of drawn-out, convoluted tasks—and, as a new employee, isn't likely to bolt at the first sign of friction.

So, absent the chance to make every job applicant work as hard as a college applicant, is there some quick, clever, cheap way of weeding out bad employees before they are hired?

Zappos has come up with one such trick. You will recall from the last chapter that Zappos, the online shoe store, has a variety of unorthodox ideas about how a business can be run. You may also recall that its customer-service reps are central to the firm's success. So even though the job might pay only $11 an hour, Zappos wants to know that each new employee is fully committed to the company's ethos. That's where "The Offer" comes in. When new employees are in the onboarding period—they've already been screened, offered a job, and completed a few weeks of training—Zappos offers them a chance to quit. Even better, quitters will be paid for their training time and also get a bonus representing their first month's salary—roughly $2,000—just for quitting! All they have to do is go through an exit interview and surrender their eligibility to be rehired at Zappos.

Doesn't that sound nuts? What kind of company would offer a new employee $2,000 to *not* work?

A clever company. "It's really putting the employee in the position of 'Do you care more about money or do you care more about this culture and the company?'" says Tony Hsieh, the company's CEO. "And if they care more about the easy money, then we probably aren't the right fit for them."

Hsieh figured that any worker who would take the easy $2,000 was the kind of worker who would end up costing Zappos a lot more in the long run. By one industry estimate, it costs an average of roughly $4,000 to replace a single employee, and one recent survey of 2,500 companies found that a single bad hire can cost more than $25,000 in lost productivity, lower morale, and the like. So Zappos decided to pay a measly $2,000 up front and let the bad hires weed themselves out before they took root. As of this writing, fewer than 1 percent of new hires at Zappos accept "The Offer."

The Zappos weeding mechanism is plainly different

from those employed by medieval priests, David Lee Roth, and King Solomon. In this case, Zappos is operating with utter transparency; there is no trick whatsoever. The other cases are all about the trick. It is the trick that makes one party reveal himself, unaware that he is being manipulated. The Zappos story therefore may strike you as more virtuous. But using a trick is—let's be honest—more fun. Consider the case of a secret bullet factory in Israel.

After World War II, the British government declared it would relinquish its rule of Palestine. Britain was depleted from the war and weary of refereeing the fractious coexistence of Arabs and Jews.

For the Jews living in Palestine, it seemed inevitable that a war with their Arab neighbors would break out as soon as the British left. So the Jewish paramilitary group Haganah began to stockpile arms. Guns were not in terribly short supply—they could be smuggled in from Europe and elsewhere—but bullets were, and it was illegal to manufacture them under British rule. So the Haganah decided to build a clandestine bullet factory on a hilltop kibbutz near Rehovot, some fifteen miles from Tel Aviv. Its code name: The Ayalon Institute.

The kibbutz had a citrus grove, a vegetable farm, and a bakery. The Institute would be located in the secret basement of a laundry building. The laundry was meant to drown out the noise of bullet-making and provide a cover story: kibbutz workers reported there for work and then, pushing aside one of the huge washing machines, descended a ladder to the factory below. Using equipment bought in Poland and smuggled in, the Institute began cranking out 9-millimeter bullets for the Sten submachine gun.

The bullet factory was so secret that women who worked there weren't allowed to tell their husbands what they were doing. The operation had to be hidden from not only the Arabs but the British too. This was especially tricky since British soldiers stationed nearby liked to have their laundry done at the kibbutz. They also dropped by to socialize— some of the kibbutzniks had fought alongside the British during World War II, as members of the Jewish Brigade.

Already there had been one close call: a British officer showed up just as a bullet-making machine was being lowered through the floor into the factory. "The fellows escorted him into the dining hall, served him beer, and we managed to get the machine down, close the opening, and conceal it," the former plant manager recalled.

Still, they were rattled. Had the British officer not been tempted by a glass of beer, the Institute likely would have been shut down, its ringleaders sent to prison. They needed to protect against another surprise visit.

The solution, the story goes, was in the beer. The British officers had complained that the beer at the kibbutz was too warm; they preferred it chilled. Their Jewish friends, eager to please, made a proposal: *The next time you plan to visit, call us beforehand and we will put some beer on ice for you.* Done and done! According to kibbutz legend at least, this warm-beer alarm worked like a charm: the British officers never again pulled a surprise visit to the factory, which went on to produce more than two million bullets for use in Israel's War of Independence. The kibbutzniks had cannily appealed to the Brits' narrow self-interest in order to satisfy their own much broader one.

There are plainly a variety of ways to teach a garden to weed itself (or, if you prefer, to create a separating equilibrium). The secret bullet factory and Zappos each dangled some bait—cold beer in one case, $2,000 in the other—that helped sort things out. The priestly ordeals relied on the threat of an omniscient God. David Lee Roth and King Solomon, meanwhile, each had to make themselves look bad in order to flush out the truth—Roth by posing as an even bigger prima donna than he was and Solomon by suggesting he was a bloodthirsty tyrant, eager to settle a maternity dispute by hacking the baby to pieces.

The method notwithstanding, seducing people to sort themselves into different categories can be all sorts of useful. It can also be extraordinarily profitable. Consider the following e-mail:

> *Dear Sir/Madam, TOP SECRET:*
>
> *I am one of the officials in the Energy management board in Lagos, Nigeria. I got your information in a business directory from the Chamber of Commerce and Industries when I was searching for a RELIABLE,*

HONEST, AND TRUSTWORTHY person to entrust this business with.

During the award of a contract to bring Electrification to Urban centres, a few of my colleagues and I had inflated the amount of this contract. The OVER-INVOICED AMOUNT is being safeguarded under our custody.

However, we have decided to transfer this sum of money, $10.3 million USA Dollars, out of Nigeria. Hence, we seek for a reliable, honest and not greedy foreign partner whom we shall use his or her account to transferring the fund. And we agreed that THE AC-COUNT OWNER SHALL BENEFIT 30% of the total amount of money.

If you are capable to handle the transaction without hitches and flaws, then we have confidence in the deal. Please, make it TOP SECRET and avoid every channel of implicating us here thereby endanger our career.

If this is of interest to you please do contact me immediately through this email address for more details and for easier communication.

Have you ever received an e-mail like this? Of course you have! There is probably one worming its way into your in-box at this very moment. If not from a government official, it purports to be from a deposed prince or a billionaire's widow. In each case, the author has the rights to millions of dollars but needs help extracting it from a rigid bureaucracy or uncooperative bank.

That's where you come in. If you will send along *your*

bank-account information (and perhaps a few sheets of blank letterhead from said bank), the widow or prince or government official can safely park the money in your account until everything is straightened out. There is a chance you will need to travel to Africa to handle the sensitive paperwork. You may also need to advance a few thousand dollars to cover some up-front fees. You will of course be richly rewarded for your trouble.

Does such an offer tempt you? We hope not. It is a stone-cold scam, variations of which have been practiced for centuries. An early version was known as the Spanish Prisoner. The scammer pretended to be a wealthy person who'd been wrongly jailed and cut off from his riches. A huge reward awaited the hero who would pay for his release. In the old days, the con was played via postal letter or face-to-face meetings; today it lives primarily on the Internet.

The generic name for this crime is advance-fee fraud, but it is more commonly called the Nigerian letter fraud or 419 fraud, after a section of the Nigerian criminal code. While advance-fee fraud is practiced in many places, Nigeria seems to be its epicenter: more e-mail scams of this sort invoke Nigeria than all other countries combined. Indeed, the connection is so famous that if you type "Nigeria" into a search engine, the auto-fill function will likely supply you with "Nigerian scam."

Which might lead you to wonder: If the Nigerian scam is so famous, why would a Nigerian scammer ever admit he is from Nigeria?

That was the question Cormac Herley asked himself. Herley is a computer scientist at Microsoft Research who has long been interested in how fraudsters abuse technology. In a previous job, at Hewlett-Packard, one of his concerns was that increasingly sophisticated desktop printers could be used to counterfeit money.

Herley hadn't thought much about the Nigerian scam until he heard two people mention it from opposite angles. One talked about the millions or even billions of dollars the scammers earn. (Firm numbers are hard to come by, but Nigerian scammers have been successful enough for the U.S. Secret Service to set up a task force; one California victim lost $5 million.) The other person noted how stupid these Nigerians must be to send out letters full of such outlandish stories and leaps of illogic.

Herley wondered how both of these statements could be true. If the scammers are so dumb and their letters so obviously a scam, how could they be successful? "When you see an apparent contradiction," he says, "you start digging, see if you can figure out a mechanism by which it *does* make sense."

He began to examine the scam from the scammers' perspective. For anyone wishing to commit fraud, the Internet has been a wondrous gift. It makes it easy to obtain a huge batch of e-mail addresses and instantaneously send out millions of bait letters. So the cost of contacting potential victims is incredibly low.

But converting a potential victim into a real one will require a good deal of time and effort—typically a long series of e-mails, perhaps some phone calls, and ultimately the bank paperwork.

Let's say for every 10,000 scam e-mails you send, 100 people take the initial bait and write back. The 9,900 who trashed your e-mail haven't cost you anything. But now you start to invest significantly in those 100 potential victims. For every one of them who wises up or gets scared off or simply loses interest, your profit margin decreases.

How many of these 100 will end up actually paying you? Let's say one of them goes all the way. The other 99 are, in the parlance of statistics, *false positives*.

Internet fraud is hardly the only realm haunted by false positives. Roughly 95 percent of the burglar alarms that U.S. police respond to are false alarms. That makes for a total of 36 million false positives a year, at a cost of nearly $2 billion. In medicine, we rightly worry about false negatives—a fatal ailment, for instance, that goes undetected—but false positives are also a huge problem. One study found an astonishingly high rate of false positives (60 percent for men, 49 percent for women) among patients who were regularly screened for prostate, lung, colorectal, or ovarian cancer. One task force went so far as to argue that ovarian screening for healthy women should be eliminated entirely since it's not very effective to begin with and because false positives lead too many women "to unnecessary harms, such as major surgery."

One of the most disruptive false positives in recent

memory occurred in Cormac Herley's own field of computer security. In 2010, the McAfee antivirus software identified a malevolent file on vast fleets of computers running Microsoft Windows. It promptly attacked the file, either deleting or quarantining it, depending on how a given computer was configured. Only one problem: the file *wasn't* malevolent—and, in fact, was a key component of the Windows start-up function. The antivirus software, by falsely attacking a healthy file, sent "millions of PC's into never-ending reboot cycles," says Herley.

So how can a Nigerian scammer minimize his false positives?

Herley used his mathematical and computing skills to model this question. Along the way, he identified the most valuable characteristic in a potential victim: gullibility. After all, who else but a supremely gullible person would send thousands of dollars to a faraway stranger based on a kooky letter about some misbegotten fortune?

How can a Nigerian scammer tell, just by looking at thousands of e-mail addresses, who is gullible and who is not? He can't. Gullibility is in this case an *unobservable trait*. But, Herley realized, the scammer can invite the gullible people to reveal themselves. How?

By sending out such a ridiculous letter—including prominent mentions of Nigeria—that only a gullible person would take it seriously. Anyone with an ounce of sense or experience would immediately trash an e-mail like this. "The scammer wants to find the guy who *hasn't* heard of it," Herley says. "Anybody who doesn't fall off their chair laughing is exactly who he wants to talk to."

Here's how Herley put it in a research paper: "The goal of the e-mail is not so much to attract viable users as to repel the non-viable ones, who greatly outnumber them. . . . A less-outlandish wording that did not mention Nigeria would almost certainly gather more total responses and more viable responses, but would yield lower overall profit. . . . [T]hose who are fooled for a while but then figure it out, or who balk at the last hurdle, are precisely the expensive false positives that the scammer must deter."

If your first instinct was to think that Nigerian scammers are stupid, perhaps you have been convinced, as Cormac Herley was, that this is exactly the kind of stupid we should all aspire to be. Their ridiculous e-mails are in fact quite brilliant at getting the scammers' massive garden to weed itself.

That said, these men are crooks and thieves. As much as one might admire their methodology, it's hard to celebrate their mission. And so now that we understand how their game works, is there a way to turn their methodology against them?

Herley believes there is. He notes with approval a small online community of "scambaiters" who intentionally engage Nigerian scammers in time-wasting e-mail conversations. "They do this mostly for bragging rights," he says. Herley would like to see this effort broadened by automation. "What you want is to build a chatbot," he says, "a computer program that can have a conversation with you. There are examples out there—there's a chatbot psychotherapist, for instance. You'd want to build something that engages the scammer on the other side, pulls him in a bit. You don't need to keep him talking for 20 round-trip e-mails, but if every time he has to put in some effort, that'd be great."

In other words, Herley would like to see a smart computer programmer pretend to be dumb in order to outwit a smart scammer who is also pretending to be dumb in order to find a victim who is, if not dumb, then extremely gullible.

Herley's chatbot would flood a scammer's system with false positives, making it virtually impossible to pick out a real victim. You might think of it as carpet-bombing the scammers' gardens with millions upon millions of weeds.

We too thought it might be nice to attack some bad guys before they were able to attack innocent people.

In *SuperFreakonomics*, published in 2009, we described an algorithm that we built with a fraud officer at a large British bank. It was designed to sift through trillions of data points generated by millions of bank customers to identify potential terrorists. It was inspired by the irregular banking behavior of the 9/11 terrorists in the United States. Among the key behaviors:

- They tended to make a large initial deposit and then steadily withdraw cash over time, with no steady replenishment.

- Their banking didn't reflect normal living expenses like rent, utilities, insurance, and so on.

- Some of them routinely sent or received foreign wire transfers, but the amount invariably fell below the reporting limit.

Markers like these are hardly enough to identify a terrorist, or even a petty criminal. But by starting with them, and culling more significant markers from the British banking data, we were able to tighten the algorithm's noose.

And tight it had to be. Imagine that our algorithm turned out to be 99 percent accurate at predicting that a given bank customer was connected to a terrorist group. That sounds pretty good until you consider the consequences of a false-positive rate of 1 percent in a case like this.

Terrorists are relatively rare in the United Kingdom. Let's say there are 500 of them. An algorithm that is 99 percent accurate would flush out 495 of them—but it would also wrongly identify 1 percent of the other people in the data. Across the entire population of the U.K., roughly 50 million adults, that would translate into some 500,000 innocent people. What would happen if you hauled in half a million non-terrorists on terrorism charges? You could brag all you wanted about how low a false-positive rate of 1 percent is— just look at the false positives that Nigerian scammers have to deal with!—but you'd still have a lot of angry people (and, likely, lawsuits) on your hands.

So the algorithm had to be closer to 99.999 percent accurate. That's what we strove for as we loaded the algorithm with marker upon marker. Some were purely demographic (known terrorists in the U.K. are predominantly young, male, and, at this point in history, Muslim). Others were behavioral. For instance: a potential terrorist was unlikely to withdraw money from an ATM on a Friday afternoon, during Muslim prayer services.

One marker, we noted, was particularly powerful in the algorithm: life insurance. A budding terrorist almost never bought life insurance from his bank, even if he had a wife and young children. Why not? As we explained in the book, an insurance policy might not pay out if the holder commits a suicide bombing, so it would be a waste of money.

After several years of tightening and tweaking, the algorithm was unleashed on a mammoth trove of banking data. It ran all night on the bank's supercomputer so as to not disturb regular business. The algorithm seemed to work pretty well. It generated a relatively short list of names that we were quite sure included at least a handful of likely terrorists. The bank gave us this list in an envelope protected by a wax seal—privacy law prevented us from seeing the names—and we in turn met with the head of a British national-security unit to hand him the envelope. It was all very James Bond-y.

What happened to the people on that list? We'd like to tell you, but we can't—not because of national-security issues but because we have no idea. While the British authorities seemed happy to take our list of names, they didn't feel compelled to let us tag along when—or if—they went knocking on suspects' doors.

That would seem to be the end of the story. But it's not.

In *SuperFreakonomics,* we described not only how the algorithm was built but how a would-be terrorist could escape its reach: by going down to the bank and buying some life insurance. The particular bank we'd been working with, we noted, "offers starter policies for just a few quid per month." We called further attention to this strategy in the book's subtitle: *Global Cooling, Patriotic Prostitutes, and Why Suicide Bombers Should Buy Life Insurance.*

Upon arrival in London for a book tour, we found the British public did not appreciate our giving advice to terrorists. "I'm not sure why we're telling the terrorists this secret," wrote one newspaper critic. Radio and TV interviewers were less polite. They asked us to explain what sort of idiot would go to the trouble of building a trap like this only to explain precisely how to evade it. Plainly we were dumber than even a Nigerian scammer, vainer than David Lee Roth, more bloodthirsty than King Solomon.

We hemmed, we hawed, we rationalized; occasionally we hung our heads in contrition. But we were smiling on the inside. And we got a little happier every time we were blasted for our stupidity. Why?

From the outset of the project, we recognized that finding a few bad apples out of millions would be difficult. Our odds would improve if we could somehow trick the bad apples into revealing themselves. That is what our life-insurance scam—yes, it was a scam all along—was meant to accomplish.

Do you know anyone who buys life insurance through their bank? No, we don't either. Many banks do offer it, but most customers use banks for straight banking and, if they want insurance, they buy it through a broker or directly from an insurer.

So as these American idiots were being skewered in the British media for giving advice to terrorists, what kind of person suddenly had a strong incentive to run out and buy life insurance from his bank? Someone who wanted to cover his tracks. And our algorithm was already in place, paying careful attention. Having learned from the great minds described in this chapter, we laid out a trap designed to ensnare only the guilty. It encouraged them to, in the words of King Solomon, "ambush only themselves."

CHAPTER 8

How to Persuade People Who Don't Want to Be Persuaded

Anyone willing to think like a Freak will occasionally end up on the sharp end of someone else's stick.

Perhaps you'll raise an uncomfortable question, challenge an orthodoxy, or simply touch upon a subject that should have been left untouched. As a result, people may call you names. They may accuse you of consorting with witches or communists or even economists. You may be heading toward a bruising fight. What happens next?

Our best advice would be to simply smile and change the subject. As hard as it is to think creatively about problems and come up with solutions, in our experience it is even harder to persuade people who do not wish to be persuaded.

But if you *are* hell-bent on persuading someone, or if your back is truly against the wall, you might as well give it your best shot. Though we try to avoid fights, we have gotten into a few, and we've learned some things along the way.

First, understand how hard persuasion will be—and why.

The vast majority of climate scientists believe the world is getting hotter, due in part to human activity, and that global warming carries a significant risk. But the American public is far less concerned. Why?

A group of researchers called the Cultural Cognition Project, made up primarily of legal scholars and psychologists, tried to answer that question.

The CCP's general mission is to determine how the public forms its views on touchy subjects like gun laws, nanotechnology, and date rape. In the case of global warming, CCP began with the possible explanation that the public just doesn't think climate scientists know what they're talking about.

But that explanation didn't fit very well. A 2009 Pew poll shows that scientists in the United States are extremely well regarded, with 84 percent of respondents calling their effect on society "mostly positive." And since scientists have thought long and hard about global warming, collecting and analyzing data, they would seem to be in a good position to know the facts.

So maybe ignorance is the answer. Perhaps the people

who aren't worried about climate change simply "aren't smart enough," as one CCP researcher posited, "they're not educated enough, they don't understand the facts like the scientists do." This explanation looked more promising. The same Pew poll found that 85 percent of scientists believe the "public does not know very much about science" and that this is a "major problem."

To determine if scientific ignorance could explain the public's lack of concern, the CCP ran its own survey. It began with questions to test each respondent's scientific and numerical literacy.

Here are some of the numerical questions:

1. Imagine that we roll a fair, six-sided die 1,000 times. (That would mean that we roll one die from a pair of dice.) Out of 1,000 rolls, how many times do you think the die would come up as an even number?

2. A bat and a ball cost $1.10 in total. The bat costs $1.00 more than the ball. How much does the ball cost?

And here are a few of the science questions:

1. *True or false:* The center of the earth is very hot.

2. *True or false:* It is the father's gene that decides whether the baby is a boy.

3. *True or false:* Antibiotics kill viruses as well as bacteria.*

After the quiz, respondents were asked another set of questions, including this one:

How much risk do you believe climate change poses to human health, safety, or prosperity?

How would you predict the survey turned out? Wouldn't you expect that people with a better grip on math and science were more likely to appreciate the threat of climate change?

Yes, that is what the CCP researchers expected too. But that's not what happened. "On the whole," the researchers concluded, "the most scientifically literate and numerate subjects were slightly *less* likely, not more, to see climate change as a serious threat than the least scientifically literate and numerate ones."

How could this be? Digging deeper, the CCP researchers found another surprise in the data. People who did well on the math and science quiz were more likely to hold an *ex-*

---

* Here are the answers to the numeracy questions, followed by the percentage of respondents who answered them correctly. (1) 500 (58 percent). (2) 5 cents (12 percent). (This question is plainly trickier than it appears. If it tripped you up—you likely thought the ball cost 10 cents—go back and read it again, focusing on the word *more*.) And now the science questions: (1) True (86 percent). (2) True (69 percent). (3) False (68 percent).

treme view of climate change in one direction or another—
that is, to consider it either gravely dangerous or wildly
overblown.

This seems odd, doesn't it? People with higher science
and math scores are presumably better educated, and we all
know that education creates enlightened, moderate people,
not extremists—don't we? Not necessarily. Terrorists, for
example, tend to be significantly better educated than their
non-terrorist peers. As the CCP researchers discovered, so
do climate-change extremists.

How can this be explained?

One reason may be that smart people simply have more
experience with feeling they are right, and therefore have
greater confidence in their knowledge, whatever side of an
issue they're on. But being confident you are right is not the
same as being right. Think back to what Philip Tetlock, who
studies the predictive ability of political pundits, found to
be a sure sign of a bad predictor: dogmatism.

Climate change may also be one of those topics that
most people just don't think about very much, or very hard.
This is understandable. The year-to-year fluctuations in climate can swamp the subtler long-term trends; the changes
will happen over decades or centuries. People are too busy
with everyday life to wrestle with something so complex
and uncertain. And so, based on their emotion or instinct,
and perhaps a reaction to a bit of information gleaned long
ago, people chose a position and stuck with it.

When someone is heavily invested in his or her opinion,

it is inevitably hard to change the person's mind. So you might think it would be pretty easy to change the minds of people who *haven't* thought very hard about an issue. But we've seen no evidence of this. Even on a topic that people don't care much about, it can be hard to get their attention long enough to prompt a change.

Richard Thaler and Cass Sunstein, pioneers of the "nudge" movement, recognized this dilemma. Rather than try to persuade people of the worthiness of a goal—whether it's conserving energy or eating better or saving more for retirement—it's more productive to essentially trick people with subtle cues or new default settings. Trying to keep a public men's room clean? Sure, go ahead and put up signs urging people to pee neatly—or, better, paint a housefly on the urinal and watch the male instinct for target practice take over.

So what does all this mean if you desperately want to persuade someone who doesn't want to be persuaded?

The first step is to appreciate that your opponent's opinion is likely based less on fact and logic than on ideology and herd thinking. If you were to suggest this to his face, he would of course deny it. He is operating from a set of biases he cannot even see. As the behavioral sage Daniel Kahneman has written: "[W]e can be blind to the obvious, and we are also blind to our blindness." Few of us are immune to this blind spot. That goes for you, and that goes for the two of us as well. And so, as the basketball legend-cum-philosopher Kareem Abdul-Jabbar once put it, "It's easier to jump out of a plane—hopefully with a parachute—than it is to change your mind about an opinion."

Okay, so how *can* you build an argument that might actually change a few minds?

It's not me; it's you.

Whenever you set out to persuade someone, remember that you are merely the producer of the argument. The consumer has the only vote that counts. Your argument may be factually indisputable and logically airtight but if it doesn't resonate for the recipient, you won't get anywhere. U.S. Congress recently funded a national, multiyear media campaign to discourage young people from using drugs. It was created by a storied ad agency and promoted by a top-tier PR firm, at a cost of nearly $1 billion. So how much do you think the campaign cut youth drug use—10 percent? Twenty? Fifty? Here's what the *American Journal of Public Health* found: "Most analyses showed no effects from the campaign" and there was in fact "some evidence that the campaign had pro-marijuana effects."

Don't pretend your argument is perfect.

Show us a "perfect" solution and we'll show you our pet unicorn. If you make an argument that promises all benefits and no costs, your opponent will never buy it—nor should he. Panaceas are almost nonexistent. If you paper over the shortcomings of your plan, that only gives your opponent reason to doubt the rest of it.

Let's say you've become a head-over-heels advocate for a new technology you think will change the world. Your argument goes like this:

> The era of the self-driving car—a.k.a. the driverless car, or autonomous vehicle—is just around the corner, and we should embrace it as vigorously as possible. It will save millions of lives and improve just about every facet of our society and economy.

You could go on and on. You could talk about how the toughest challenge—the technology itself—has largely been conquered. Nearly every major automaker in the world, as well as Google, has successfully tested cars that use an onboard computer, GPS, cameras, radar, laser scanners, and actuators to do everything a human driver can do—but better. And since roughly 90 percent of the world's 1.2 million traffic deaths each year—yes, *1.2 million deaths*, every year!—are the result of driver error, the driverless car may be one of the biggest lifesavers in recent history. Unlike humans, a driverless car won't drive drowsy or drunk, or while texting or applying mascara; it won't change lanes while putting ketchup on french fries or turn around to smack its kids in the backseat.

Google has already driven its fleet of autonomous cars more than 500,000 miles on real roads throughout the United States without causing an accident.* But safety isn't the only benefit. Elderly and handicapped people wouldn't have to drive themselves to the doctor (or, if they prefer, to the beach). Parents wouldn't have to worry about their reckless teenagers getting behind the wheel. People could drink without hesitation when they go out at night—good news for restaurants, bars, and the alcohol industry. Since a driverless car can flow through traffic more efficiently, road congestion and pollution would likely fall. And if driverless cars could be summoned to pick us up or drop us off, we'd no longer need to park at our destination, freeing up millions of acres of prime real estate. In many U.S. cities, 30 to 40 percent of the downtown surface area is devoted to parking.

Well, that all sounds pretty perfect, doesn't it?

But of course no new technology is perfect, especially something as vast as a driverless-car revolution. So if you want your argument to be taken seriously, you'd do well to admit the potential downsides.

For starters, the technology may be miraculous but it is still in the experimental phase and may never be as good

---

* In the accumulation of those 500,000 miles, Google's driverless cars *were* involved in two accidents, but in each case, the car was not in self-driving mode and was being operated by a human. In the first accident, the Google car was rear-ended at a stoplight; in the second, the Google driver got into a fender-bender while manually driving the car.

as promised. True, the sensors on a driverless car can easily distinguish a pedestrian from a tree, but there are many other issues to surmount. Google's engineers concede this: "[W]e'll need to master snow-covered roadways, interpret temporary construction signals and handle other tricky situations that many drivers encounter."

There will be countless legal, liability, and practical roadblocks, including the fact that many people may never trust a computer to drive them or their loved ones.

And what about all the people who drive for a living? Nearly 3 percent of the U.S. workforce—about 3.6 million people—feed their families by driving taxis, buses, delivery trucks, tractor-trailers, and other vehicles. What are they supposed to do when this new technology obliterates their livelihood?

What else might go wrong in a driverless future? It's hard to say. The future, as we have noted, is nearly impossible to predict. This doesn't stop a lot of policymakers and technologists from pretending otherwise. They constantly ask us to assume that their latest projects—whether a piece of legislation or a piece of software—will perform exactly as it was drawn up. It rarely does. So if you want your argument to be truly persuasive, it's a good idea to acknowledge not only the known flaws but the potential for unintended consequences. For instance:

As the hassle and cost of driving fall, will we use driverless cars so much that they produce even *more* congestion and pollution?

With drunk driving no longer a worry, will we see a worldwide deluge of binge drinking?

Wouldn't a fleet of computer-controlled cars be vulnerable to hacking, and what happens when some cyber-terrorist steers every vehicle west of the Mississippi into the Grand Canyon?

And what if, on one beautiful spring day, a mis-programmed car plows through a playground and kills a dozen schoolchildren?

Acknowledge the strengths of your opponent's argument.

If you are trying to persuade someone, why on earth would you want to lend credence to his argument?

One reason is that the opposing argument almost certainly has value—something you can learn from and use to strengthen your own argument. This may seem hard to believe since you are so invested in your argument, but remember: we are blind to our blindness.

Furthermore, an opponent who feels his argument is ignored isn't likely to engage with you at all. He may shout at you and you may shout back at him, but it is hard to persuade someone with whom you can't even hold a conversation.

Think back to the driverless car that just mowed down a flock of schoolchildren. Is there any value in pretending that such accidents won't happen? None that we can think of. The death of these children would horrify everyone who heard about it; for the victims' parents, the very idea of a driverless car would become repugnant.

But let's consider a different set of parents: the ones whose children are currently dying in traffic accidents. Around the world, some 180,000 kids are killed each year, or roughly 500 a day. In wealthy countries, this is easily the leading cause of death for kids from ages five to fourteen, outpacing the next four causes—leukemia, drowning, violence, and self-inflicted injuries—*combined*. In the United States alone, traffic accidents kill more than 1,100 kids, age fourteen and under, each year, with another 171,000 injuries.

How many children's lives would a driverless car save? That's impossible to say. Some advocates predict it would nearly eliminate traffic deaths over time. But let's assume that is way too optimistic. Let's say the driverless car would lower the death toll by 20 percent. That would save 240,000 lives around the world every year, including 36,000 children. Thirty-six thousand sets of parents who wouldn't have to grieve! And death is just a part of it. Roughly 50 million people a year are injured or disabled by traffic accidents, and the financial cost is mind-boggling: more than half a trillion dollars annually. How nice it would be to lower those numbers by "only" 20 percent.

So yes, we should acknowledge the heartbreak of the parents whose kids were killed when that driverless car ran amok in the playground. But we should also acknowledge how inured we've become to the heartbreak faced by millions of people every day because of car crashes.

How did this happen? Maybe we simply accept the trade-off because the car is such a wonderful and necessary part of life. Or maybe it's because traffic deaths are so commonplace—most of them barely make the news—that, unlike the rare, noisy events that do capture our attention, we just don't think about them.

In July 2013, an Asiana Airlines flight from South Korea crashed at the San Francisco airport, resulting in three deaths. The crash got big play on just about every media outlet in the country. The message was clear: air travel can be deadly. But how does it compare with car travel? Before the Asiana crash, it had been more than four years since the last fatal commercial flight in the United States. During this period of zero airline deaths, more than 140,000 Americans died in traffic crashes.*

What kind of person could possibly object to a new technology that saves even a fraction of those lives? You'd have to be a misanthrope, a troglodyte, or at the very least a pure idiot.

---

* As vast as the difference is between car and airplane deaths, we should point out that there is not quite as much variance in the death rate per mile, as people travel considerably more miles in cars than on planes. In a given year, drivers in the United States cover nearly 3 trillion miles (and that doesn't include the miles ridden by passengers) while airline passengers in the States fly about 570 billion (or .57 trillion) miles.

Keep the insults to yourself.

Uh-oh. Now you've gone and called your opponents a bunch of misanthropes, troglodytes, and idiots. Have we mentioned that name-calling is a really bad idea if you want to persuade someone who doesn't wish to be persuaded? For evidence, look no further than the U.S. Congress, which in recent years has operated less like a legislative body than a deranged flock of summer campers locked in an endless color war.

Human beings, for all our accomplishments, can be fragile animals. Most of us don't take criticism well at all. A spate of recent research shows that negative information "weighs more heavily on the brain," as one research team put it. A second team makes an even starker claim: in the human psyche, "bad is stronger than good." This means that negative events—vicious crimes, horrible accidents, and sundry dramatic evils—make an outsize impression on our memories. This may explain why we are so bad at assessing risk, and so quick to overrate rare dangers (like an airplane crash in San Francisco that kills three people). It also means that the pain of negative feedback will for most people trump the pleasure from positive feedback.

Consider a recent study of German schoolteachers. As it happens, teachers are far more likely to take early retirement than other public employees in Germany, with the chief culprit being poor mental health. A team of medical researchers tried to determine the cause of all this poor mental health. They analyzed many factors: teaching load and class size as well as each teacher's interactions with colleagues, students, and parents. One factor emerged as the best predictor of poor mental health: whether a teacher had been verbally insulted by his or her students.

So if you are hoping to damage opponents' mental health, go ahead and tell them how inferior or dim-witted or nasty they are. But even if you are certifiably right on every point, you should not think for a minute that you will ever be able to persuade them. Name-calling will make you an enemy, not an ally, and if that is your objective, then persuasion is probably not what you were after in the first place.

Why you should tell stories.

We have saved for last the most powerful form of persuasion we know. Sure, it's important to acknowledge the flaws in your argument and keep the insults to yourself, but if you really want to persuade someone who doesn't wish to be persuaded, you should tell him a story.

By "story," we don't mean "anecdote." An anecdote is a snapshot, a one-dimensional shard of the big picture. It is lacking in scale, perspective, and data. (As scientists like to say: *The plural of anecdote is not data.*) An anecdote is something that once happened to you, or to your uncle, or to your uncle's accountant. It is too often an outlier, the memorable exception that gets trotted out in an attempt to disprove a larger truth. *My uncle's accountant drives drunk all the time, and he's never even had a fender-bender—so how dangerous can drunk driving be?* Anecdotes often represent the lowest form of persuasion.

A story, meanwhile, fills out the picture. It uses data, statistical or otherwise, to portray a sense of magnitude; without data, we have no idea how a story fits into the larger scheme of things. A good story also includes the passage of time, to show the degree of constancy or change; without a time frame, we can't judge whether we're looking at something truly noteworthy or just an anomalous blip. And a story lays out a daisy chain of events, to show the causes that lead up to a particular situation and the consequences that result from it.

Alas, not all stories are true. A great deal of conventional wisdom is built on nothing more than a story that someone has been telling for so long—often out of self-interest—that it is treated like gospel. So it is always worth questioning what a story is based on, and what it really means.

Here's a story, for instance, that we've all heard for many years: the obesity epidemic is the result of too many people eating too much fatty food. That sounds right, doesn't it? If *being* fat is a bad thing, then *eating* fat must also be bad. Why would they give the same name to the nutritional component and the state of being overweight if the component didn't cause the state? This is the story that launched a million low-fat diets and products, with the U.S. government often leading the way.

But is it true?

There are at least two problems with this story: (1) an ever-growing body of evidence suggests that eating fat is pretty good for us, at least certain types of fat and in moderation; and (2) when people stopped eating fat, it wasn't as if they instead ate nothing; they began to consume more sugar and more carbohydrates that the body turns into sugar—and which, the evidence suggests, is a huge contributor to obesity.

It is a testament to the power of storytelling that even stories that aren't true can be so persuasive. That said, we encourage you to use as generous a portion of the truth as possible in your attempts to persuade.

Why are stories so valuable?

One reason is that a story exerts a power beyond the obvious. The whole is so much greater than the sum of the parts—the facts, the events, the context—that a story creates a deep resonance.

Stories also appeal to the narcissist in all of us. As a story unspools, with its cast of characters moving through time and making decisions, we inevitably put ourselves in their shoes. *Yes, I would have done that too!* or *No no no, I never would have made that decision!*

Perhaps the best reason to tell stories is simply that they capture our attention and are therefore good at teaching. Let's say there's a theory or concept or set of rules you need to convey. While some people have the capacity to latch on directly to a complex message—we are talking to you, engineers and computer scientists—most of us quickly zone out if a message is too clinical or technical.

This was the problem faced by Steve Epstein, who at the time was a lawyer for the U.S. Department of Defense. As head of the Standards of Conduct Office, Epstein had to brief supervisors in various government departments on the sort of things their employees were and were not allowed to do. "And the problem of course is keeping that training fresh, keeping it relevant," Epstein says. "And to do that we discovered that the first thing you have to do is you have to entertain folks enough so they will pay attention."

Epstein discovered that straightforward recitation of the rules and regulations wouldn't work. So he created a book of true stories called *The Encyclopedia of Ethical Failure*. It is a catalog of the epic screw-ups perpetrated by federal workers, divided into helpful chapters like "Abuse of Position," "Bribery," "Conflicts of Interest," and "Political Activity Violations." The *Encyclopedia* is one of the most entertaining publications in U.S. government history (which, to be fair, isn't saying much). We hear about the "entrepreneurial Federal employee" who "backed his panel van up to the office door one night and stole all the computer equipment" and then "tried to sell everything at a yard sale the next day." We learn that "a military officer was reprimanded for faking his own death to end an affair." Then there's the Department of Defense employee who used her Pentagon office to sell real estate. (When caught, she promptly quit the DoD and went into real estate full-time.)

What the *Encyclopedia* proved, at least to Steve Epstein and his Pentagon colleagues, is that a rule makes a much stronger impression once a story illustrating said rule is lodged in your mind.

The same lesson can be learned from one of the most widely read books in history: the Bible. What is the Bible "about"? Different people will of course answer that question differently. But we could all agree the Bible contains perhaps the most influential set of rules in human history: the Ten Commandments. They became the foundation of not only the Judeo-Christian tradition but of many societies at large. So surely most of us can recite the Ten Commandments front to back, back to front, and every way in between, right?

All right then, go ahead and name the Ten Commandments. We'll give you a minute to jog your memory . . .

. . .

. . .

. . .

Okay, here they are:

1. I am the Lord your God, who brought you out of the land of Egypt, the house of bondage.

2. You shall have no other gods before Me.

3. You shall not take the name of the Lord your God in vain.

4. Remember the Sabbath day, to make it holy.

5. Honor your father and your mother.

6. You shall not murder.

7. You shall not commit adultery.

8. You shall not steal.

9. You shall not bear false witness against your neighbor.

10. You shall not covet your neighbor's house, nor your neighbor's wife . . . nor any thing that is your neighbor's.

How did you do? Probably not so well. But don't worry—most people don't. A recent survey found that only 14 percent of U.S. adults could recall all Ten Commandments; only 71 percent could name even *one* commandment. (The three best-remembered commandments were numbers 6, 8, and 10—murder, stealing, and coveting—while number 2, forbidding false gods, was in last place.)

Maybe, you're thinking, this says less about biblical rules than how bad our memories are. But consider this: in the same survey, 25 percent of the respondents could name the seven principal ingredients of a Big Mac, while 35 percent could name all six kids from *The Brady Bunch*.

If we have such a hard time recalling the most famous

set of rules from perhaps the most famous book in history, what *do* we remember from the Bible?

The stories. We remember that Eve fed Adam a forbidden apple and that one of their sons, Cain, murdered the other, Abel. We remember that Moses parted the Red Sea in order to lead the Israelites out of slavery. We remember that Abraham was instructed to sacrifice his own son on a mountain—and we even remember that King Solomon settled a maternity dispute by threatening to slice a baby in half. These are the stories we tell again and again and again, even those of us who aren't remotely "religious." Why? Because they stick with us; they move us; they persuade us to consider the constancy and frailties of the human experience in a way that mere rules cannot.

Consider one more story from the Bible, about King David. He slept with a married woman, Bathsheba, and got her pregnant. In order to cover up his transgression, David arranged for Bathsheba's husband, a soldier, to die in battle. David then took Bathsheba as his own wife.

God sent a prophet named Nathan to let David know this behavior was unacceptable. But how does a lowly prophet go about imparting such a message to the king of Israel?

Nathan told him a story. He described to David two men, one rich and one poor. The rich man had huge flocks of animals; the poor man had just one little lamb, whom he treated like a member of his family.

One day a traveler came through. The rich man, Nathan told King David, was happy to feed the traveler but he didn't want to take a sheep from his own flock. So he took the poor man's only lamb, killed it, and served it to the traveler.

The story enrages David: "The man who did this deserves to die," he says.

"That man," Nathan tells him, "is you."

Case closed. Nathan didn't berate David with rules—*Hey, don't covet your neighbor's wife! Hey, don't kill! Hey, don't commit adultery!*—even though David had broken all of them. He just told a story about a lamb. Very persuasive.

All we've been doing in this book, really, is telling stories—about a hot-dog-eating champion, an ulcer detective, a man who wanted to give free surgery to the world's poorest children. There are of course a million variations in how a given story can be told: the ratio of narrative to data; the pace and flow and tone; the point of the narrative arc at which you "cut into" the story, as the great writer-doctor Anton Chekhov noted. We have been telling these stories in an effort to persuade you to think like a Freak. Perhaps we haven't been entirely successful, but the fact you have read this far suggests we haven't failed altogether.

In that case, we invite you to listen to one more story. It's about a classic piece of advice that just about everyone has received at one point or another—and why you should ignore it.

CHAPTER 9

The Upside of Quitting

All these years later, the words still resonate: "Never give in, never give in, never, never, never—in nothing, great or small, large or petty."

The speaker was British prime minister Winston Churchill; he was delivering remarks at Harrow, the boarding school of his youth. But this wasn't the standard pep talk given by men like him to boys like those, urging them to stick to their studies. The date was October 29, 1941, deep in the heart of World War II.

Hitler's army had been gobbling up huge swaths of Europe and beyond. Britain was its most formidable opponent—the U.S. had not yet been drawn into the war—and, accordingly, had paid the price. German warplanes had bombed Britain nonstop for months, killing tens of thousands of civilians. A German land invasion was said to be in the works.

The situation had improved of late, but it was still impossible to know whether Britain could beat back Germany, or whether Great Britain would even exist a few years hence. And so Churchill's words that day at Harrow—"never give in, never, never, never"—took on an urgency and a magnitude that inspired not only those boys on that day but millions of people for years to come.

The message is unequivocal: failure may be an option but quitting is not. The American version goes like this: "A quitter never wins, and a winner never quits." To quit is to prove oneself a coward, a shirker, a person of limited character—let's face it, a *loser*. Who could possibly argue with that?

A Freak, that's who.

Sure, if you are prime minister of a great nation that is facing extinction, fighting to the death is indeed the best option. But for the rest of us, the stakes aren't usually so high. There is in fact a huge upside to quitting when done right, and we suggest you give it a try.

You've been at it for a while now, whatever the "it" is—a job, an academic pursuit, a business start-up, a relationship, a charitable endeavor, a military career, a sport. Maybe it's a dream project you've been working on for so long you can't even remember what got you all dreamy in the first place. In your most honest moments, it's easy to see that things aren't working out. So why haven't you quit?

THE UPSIDE OF QUITTING

At least three forces bias us against quitting. The first is a lifetime of being told by Churchill wannabes that quitting is a sign of failure.

The second is the notion of *sunk costs*. This is pretty much what it sounds like: the time or money or sweat equity you've already spent on a project. It is tempting to believe that once you're invested heavily in something, it is counterproductive to quit. This is known as the *sunk-cost fallacy* or, as the biologist Richard Dawkins called it, *the Concorde fallacy,* after the supersonic airplane. Its two patrons, the British and French governments, suspected the Concorde was not economically viable but had spent too many billions to stop. In simpler times, this was known as *throwing good money after bad*—but money is hardly the only resource that people toss into the sunk-cost trap. Think about all the time, brainpower, and social or political capital you continued to spend on some commitment only because you didn't like the idea of quitting.

The third force that keeps people from quitting is a tendency to focus on concrete costs and pay too little attention to *opportunity cost*. This is the notion that for every dollar or hour or brain cell you spend on one thing, you surrender the opportunity to spend it elsewhere. Concrete costs are usually easy to calculate, but opportunity cost is harder. If you want to go back to school to get an MBA, you know it'll cost two years' time and $80,000—but what might you have done with that time and money had you not been in school? Or let's say you've been a competitive runner for years and it's still a big part of your identity—but what else might you accomplish if you weren't slamming your joints into the pavement ten hours a week? Might you do something that makes your life, or others' lives, more fulfilling, more productive, more exciting? Perhaps. If only you weren't so worried about the sunk costs. If only you could quit.

Let's be clear: we are not suggesting you quit everything in order to do *nothing,* to spend all day on the couch in your underwear, eating nachos and watching TV. But if you're stuck in a project or relationship or mind-set that isn't working, and if the opportunity cost seems to outweigh the sunk cost, here are some ways to think about the big quit.

Quitting is hard in part because it is equated with failure, and nobody likes to fail, or at least be seen failing. But is failure necessarily so terrible?

We don't think so. For every ten Freakonomics research projects we take up, roughly nine are abandoned within a month. For whatever reason, it turns out we aren't the right people to take them on. Resources are not infinite: you cannot solve tomorrow's problem if you aren't willing to abandon today's dud.

Nor should failure be considered a total loss. Once you start thinking like a Freak and running experiments, you'll find that failure can provide valuable feedback. Former New York City mayor Michael Bloomberg understood this.

"In medicine, or in science, [if] you go down a path and it turns out to be a dead end, you really made a contribution, because we know we don't have to go down that path again," he said. "In the press, they call it failure. And so people are unwilling to innovate, unwilling to take risks in government."

Civilization is an aggressive, almost maniacal chronicler of success. This is understandable—but might we all be better off if failure carried less of a stigma? Some people think so. They go so far as to celebrate their failures with a party and cake.

Intellectual Ventures is a technology firm near Seattle with an unusual mandate. I.V.'s main business is acquiring and licensing out high-tech patents, but it also runs an old-fashioned invention shop. Some inventions originate in-house while others are dreamed up in some garage on the other side of the world. The ideas range from a new breed of nuclear reactor to a superinsulated, portable storage unit that can deliver perishable vaccines to sub-Saharan Africa.

When it comes to inventing, ideas are rarely in short supply. In one brainstorming session, a group of I.V. scientists might come up with fifty ideas. "It's just a fact of invention that most ideas won't work out," says Geoff Deane, who runs I.V.'s laboratory, where viable ideas are put to the test. "Knowing when the time is right to walk away is a perpetual challenge."

The first round of triage is made by the company's army of business, technical, and legal analysts. If an idea survives that cut, it may make its way to Deane's lab, a fifty-thousand-square-foot menagerie of saws, scopes, lasers, lathes, and jacked-up computers. It employs or hosts more than one hundred people.

By the time an invention makes it to the lab, Deane says, there are two forces at work. "One force really wants to find a winner. The other one doesn't want you to spend a ton of money or time on an idea that won't be successful. The key is failing fast and failing cheap. That's a mantra that comes out of Silicon Valley. I prefer the statement 'failing well,' or 'failing smart.'"

Deane, an upbeat man with a big shaved head, has a background in civil engineering and fluid mechanics. The hardest part of running the lab, he says, "is training people to understand that risk is part of their job, and if they fail well, they will be given the license to fail again. If we try to spend ten thousand dollars on our failures instead of ten million dollars, we'll get the opportunity to do a lot more things." In this context, Deane says, failure "has to be recognized as a victory."

He recalls one invention in 2009 that looked to be a winner. It was a "self-sterilizing surface," a technology that used ultraviolet light to wipe out dangerous microbes. In U.S. hospitals alone, tens of thousands of people die each year from infections they pick up from medical devices, door handles, light switches, remote controls, and furniture surfaces. Wouldn't it be great if all those items could be treated with a coating that automatically wiped out killer bacteria?

The self-sterilizing surface took advantage of two scientific phenomena—"total internal reflection" and "evanescent field effect"—to expose microbial intruders to ultraviolet light and neutralize them. To test the concept, I.V. scientists wrote white papers and computer models, cultivated bacteria, and built prototypes. There was tremendous excitement about the project. Nathan Myhrvold, one of the company's founders, began to talk it up publicly.

How did the testing go? The self-sterilizing surface turned out to be "highly effective in killing bacteria," Deane says.

That was the good news. The bad news: the existing technology to commercialize the invention was simply too expensive. There was no way it could move forward, at least for now. "We were ahead of the curve," Deane says. "We just had to wait for the world to make more cost-effective LEDs."

Projects fail for all kinds of reasons. Sometimes the science isn't right; sometimes it is politics that gets in the way. In this case, the economics just wouldn't cooperate. But Geoff Deane felt good about the outcome. The work had gone quickly and had cost the company only $30,000. "It's very easy to have a project like that go on for six months," he says. "The technology was by no means dead, but the project needed to be put to rest for a while."

And so Deane threw an old-fashioned wake. "We invited everyone over to the kitchen, had a cake, said a few words of memoriam," he says. "Somebody had made a casket. We carried it outside—we have a grassy knoll—and we put up a tombstone." Then they all went back inside to continue the party. It was remarkably well attended—about fifty people. "When you offer free food and alcohol at the end of the day, people tend to show up," Deane says.

When failure is demonized, people will try to avoid it at all costs—even when it represents nothing more than a temporary setback.

We once consulted with a huge multinational retail chain that was planning to open its first store in China. The company's top executives were deeply committed to opening on time. About two months beforehand, they gathered the leaders of the seven teams involved in the opening, and asked each one for a detailed status report. All the reports were positive. All the team leaders were then asked to pick one of three signals—a green light, yellow light, or red light—to indicate their confidence in an on-time opening. All seven of them picked the green light. Great news!

As it happens, this firm had also set up an internal prediction market, where any employee could anonymously place a small bet on various company directives. One bet asked whether the Chinese store would open on time. Considering that all seven team leaders had given it a green light, you might expect bettors to be similarly bullish. They weren't. The prediction market showed a 92 percent chance the store *wouldn't* open on time.

Guess who was right—the anonymous bettors or the team leaders who had to stand in front of their bosses?

The Chinese store did not open on time.

It's easy to identify with the leaders who gave the project the green light. Once a boss gets "go fever," it takes a lot of courage to focus on potential failures. Institutional politics, ego, and momentum are all conspiring against you. And "go fever" can have consequences far more tragic than the late opening of a Chinese flagship store.

On January 28, 1986, NASA planned to launch the space shuttle *Challenger* from Kennedy Space Center in Cape Canaveral, Florida. The launch had already been delayed several times. The mission had drawn massive public interest, largely because the crew included a civilian, a New Hampshire schoolteacher named Christa McAuliffe.

The night before the launch, NASA held a long teleconference call with engineers from Morton Thiokol, the contractor that built the *Challenger*'s solid-rocket motors. Among them was Allan McDonald, Morton Thiokol's senior man at the launch site. It was unusually cold in Florida—a predicted overnight low of 18 degrees—so McDonald and other Morton Thiokol engineers recommended the launch be postponed again. The cold weather, they explained, might damage the rubber O-rings that kept hot gases from escaping the shuttle boosters. The boosters had never been tested below 53 degrees, and the morning forecast called for temperatures much lower than that.

On the call, NASA pushed back against McDonald's decision to postpone. He was surprised. "This was the first time that NASA personnel ever challenged a recommendation that was made that said it was *unsafe* to fly," he later wrote. "For some strange reason, we found ourselves being challenged to prove quantitatively that it would definitely fail, and we couldn't do that."

As McDonald later recalled, his boss, back at Morton Thiokol headquarters in Utah, left the phone call for roughly thirty minutes to discuss the situation with other company executives. "When Utah came back on the phone," McDonald wrote, "*somehow* the decision had been reversed." The launch was officially back on.

McDonald was livid, but he had been overruled. NASA asked Morton Thiokol to sign off on the decision to launch. McDonald refused; his boss signed instead. The next morning, the *Challenger* took off as scheduled and blew apart in midair just seventy-three seconds later, killing everyone aboard. The cause, as later established by a presidential commission, was the failure of O-rings due to the cold weather.

What makes this story remarkable—and even more tragic—is that the people in the know had forecast the exact cause of failure. You'd think it is a rare case when a group of decision makers know with such precision what the fatal flaw of a given project will be. But is it? What if there were a way to peek around the corner on any project to see if it's destined to fail—that is, if you could learn how you might fail without going to the trouble of actually failing?

That's the idea behind a "premortem," as the psychologist Gary Klein calls it. The idea is simple. Many institutions already conduct a postmortem on failed projects, hoping to learn exactly what killed the patient. A premortem tries to find out what *might* go wrong before it's too late. You gather up everyone connected with a project and have them imagine that it launched and failed miserably. Now they each write down the exact reasons for its failure. Klein has found the premortem can help flush out the flaws or doubts in a project that no one had been willing to speak aloud.

This suggests one way to make a premortem even more useful: offer anonymity.

It seems safe to say that failure is not necessarily the enemy of success, as long as it's given its due. But what about quitting outright? It's all well and good for us to preach the upside of quitting, to point out opportunity cost and the sunk-cost fallacy. But is there any actual evidence that quitting leads to better outcomes?

Carsten Wrosch, a psychology professor at Concordia University, helped run a series of small studies to see what happens when people give up "unattainable" goals. Granted, deciding whether a goal is unattainable is probably 90 percent of the battle. "Yes," Wrosch says, "I would say that's the $1 million question—when to struggle and when to quit."

In any case, Wrosch found that people who quit their unattainable goals saw physical and psychological benefits. "They have, for example, less depressive symptoms, less negative affect over time," he says. "They also have lower cortisol levels, and they have lower levels of systemic inflammation, which is a marker of immune functioning. And they develop fewer physical health problems over time."

Wrosch's research is interesting but, let's be honest, not quite the overwhelming evidence you might need to cut the cord. Whether quitting is "worth it" is the kind of question that is inevitably hard to answer, at least empirically. How are you supposed to gather the data to answer such a question?

What you'd really like to do is find thousands of people teetering on the edge of quitting, who just can't decide on the right path. Then, with one flick of a magic wand, you'd send a randomly chosen portion of those people down the quitting path while the rest carried on—and you'd get to sit back and observe how all their lives unfolded.

Unfortunately, no such wand exists. (Not that we know of, at least. Maybe Intellectual Ventures—or the NSA—is working on it.) So we tried the next best thing. We set up a website, named it Freakonomics Experiments, and asked people to put their fate in our hands. Here's what the home page said:

HAVE A PROBLEM?

Sometimes in life you face a major decision, and you just don't know what to do. You've considered the issue from every angle. But no matter how you look at it, no decision seems to be the right decision.

In the end, whatever you choose will essentially be a flip of a coin.

Help us by letting Freakonomics Experiments flip that coin for you.

That's right: we asked people to let us decide their future with a coin toss. We ensured their anonymity, asked them to tell us their dilemma, and then flipped the coin. (Technically, it was a digital coin toss from a random number generator, which ensured its fairness.) Heads meant quitting and tails meant sticking it out. We also asked them to check in with us after two months and again after six months so we could see whether quitting made them happier or less happy. And we asked for a third party—a friend or family member usually—to verify that the flipper actually followed the coin flip.

As ludicrous as this may seem, within a few months our website had attracted enough potential quitters to flip more than 40,000 coins. The male-female split was about 60-40; the average age was just under 30. Some 30 percent of the flippers were married, and 73 percent lived in the United States; the rest were scattered across the globe.

We offered a menu of decisions in a variety of categories: career, education, family, health, home, relationships, and "just for fun." Here are some of the questions that proved most popular:

> *Should I quit my job?*
> *Should I go back to school?*
> *Should I go on a diet?*
> *Should I break my bad habit?*
> *Should I break up with my boyfriend/girlfriend?*

Not all the decisions were technically a "quit." We'd flip a coin if someone couldn't decide whether to get a tattoo or start volunteering or try online dating. We also let people write in their own questions (although we did tweak the software to block some queries—anything containing "murder," "steal," or "suicide," for instance). Just to give you a flavor, here are some of the write-in questions we received:

> *Should I get out of the military?*
> *Should I quit taking illicit drugs?*
> *Should I date my boss?*
> *Should I stop stalking my love interest?*
> *Should I quit grad school?*
> *Should I have the fourth child that my husband wants?*
> *Should I quit the Mormon faith?*

Should I become a Christian?

Should I have a coronary bypass or an angioplasty?

Should I be an investment banker in London or a private-equity associate in New York?

Should I rebalance my portfolio or just let it go?

Should I redo the bathroom or finish the basement first?

Should I attend my youngest sister's wedding in North Carolina?

Should I come out?

Should I give up my dream of being a musician?

Should I sell my motorcycle?

Should I go vegan?

Should I let my talented daughter quit piano?

Should I start a Facebook Lebanese women's-rights movement?

We were astonished to see how many people were willing to put their fate in the hands of some strangers with a coin. Granted, they wouldn't have made it to our site if they weren't already leaning toward making a change. Nor could we force them to obey the coin. Overall, though, 60 percent of the people did follow the coin toss—which means that thousands of people made a choice they wouldn't have made if the toss had come out opposite.

Predictably, the coin toss had less impact on some really

big decisions, like quitting a job, but even there it had some power. People were especially willing to follow the coin's command when it came to the following questions:

Should I ask for a raise?

Should I quit my bad habit?

Should I splurge on something fun?

Should I sign up for a marathon?

Should I grow a beard or mustache?

Should I break up with my boyfriend/girlfriend?

On this last question—the romantic breakup—we were responsible for the dissolution of roughly 100 couples. (To the jilted lovers: sorry!) On the other hand, because of the nature of a coin flip, we were also responsible for keeping together another 100 couples who might have broken up had the coin landed on heads.

The experiment is ongoing and results are still coming in, but we have enough data to draw some tentative conclusions.

Some decisions, it turns out, don't seem to affect people's happiness at all. One example: growing facial hair. (We can't say this was very surprising.)

Some decisions made people considerably *less* happy: asking for a raise, splurging on something fun, and signing up for a marathon. Our data don't allow us to say *why* these choices made people unhappy. It could be that if you ask for a raise and don't get it, you feel resentful. And maybe training for a marathon is far more appealing in theory than in practice.

Some changes, meanwhile, did leave people happier, including two of the most substantial quits: breaking up with a boyfriend/girlfriend and quitting a job.

Have we definitively proven that people are on average more likely to be better off if they quit more jobs, relationships, and projects? Not by a long shot. But there is nothing in the data to suggest that quitting leads to misery either. So we hope the next time you face a tough decision, you'll keep that in mind. Or maybe you'll just flip a coin. True, it may seem strange to change your life based on a totally random event. It may seem even stranger to abdicate responsibility for your own decisions. But putting your faith in a coin toss—even for a tiny decision—may at least inoculate you against the belief that quitting is necessarily taboo.

As noted earlier, we are all slaves to our own biases. Maybe that is why the two of us are so open to quitting. We have each been serial quitters and are pretty happy about how things turned out.

One of us—Levitt, the economist—was pretty sure, from the age of nine, that he would be a professional golfer. When he wasn't practicing, he fantasized about being the next Jack Nicklaus. His progress was substantial. At age seventeen, he qualified for the Minnesota state amateur championship. But his playing partner during that qualifier—a short, squat, unathletic-looking fourteen-year-old—routinely outdrove him by thirty or forty yards and beat him soundly. *If I can't beat this kid,* he thought, *how am I ever going to be a touring pro?* The lifelong golf dream was summarily shuttered.*

Years later, he enrolled in an economics Ph.D. program not because he thought an economics career would be fun but because it gave him cover to quit a management-consulting job he hated. He focused on political economics and by any standard metric, his career was going well. Just one problem: political economics was no fun at all. Yes, it was an "important" field, but the work itself was dry as bones.

There seemed to be three options:

1. Plow on regardless.

2. Quit economics entirely and move into Mom and Dad's basement.

3. Find a new specialty within economics that wasn't so dull.

Number 1 was the easiest choice. A few more publications and our hero would likely earn tenure at a top economics department. This option exploited what academics call the *status-quo bias,* a preference for keeping things as

---

* In retrospect, Levitt may have given up too easily. That squat fourteen-year-old was Tim "Lumpy" Herron, who as of this writing is approaching his twentieth year on the PGA Tour, with career earnings of more than $18 million.

they are—and, to be sure, a prime force against quitting anything. Number 2 had some intrinsic appeal but, having already tried it once without much success, he passed. Number 3 beckoned. But was there any activity he enjoyed that might also reboot his academic career?

Indeed there was: watching *Cops* on TV. *Cops* was one of the first reality shows of the modern era.* No, it wasn't very classy, and probably not "important," but it was incredibly fun to watch. Addictive, even. Every week, viewers rode along with cops in Baltimore or Tampa or even Moscow as they chased down disorderly drunks and carjackers and wife beaters. The show wasn't remotely scientific, but it did get you thinking. *Why are so many of the criminals and the victims drunk? Does gun control really work? How much money do drug dealers make? What's more important, the number of police or the tactics they use? Does locking up a lot of criminals lower the crime rate, or just encourage new and wilder criminals to take their place?*

Watching a few dozen hours of *Cops* prompted enough questions to fuel a decade's worth of fascinating academic research. (Maybe sitting on a couch eating nachos and watching TV *isn't* so terrible!) And just like that, a new career path was laid out: the economics of crime. It was an

---

* Interestingly, the idea for *Cops* had been floating around for years but it didn't get the green light until the Writers Guild strike of 1988. Suddenly, the networks were more interested in its cinema verité. "[A] series with no narrator, no host, no script, no re-enactments sounded very good to them at the time," recalled John Langley, the show's co-creator.

underserved market and, although not nearly as important as political economics or macroeconomics or labor economics, it could permanently keep this economist out of his parents' basement. And so it was that he quit trying to be an important economist.

The second author of this book has quit both a childhood dream and a dream job. He played music from an early age, and in college helped start a rock band, The Right Profile, named for a song on the Clash record *London Calling*. Ragged at first, they improved over time. On their best days, they sounded like a rough mashup of the Rolling Stones, Bruce Springsteen, and some country punks who didn't know any better. After a few years, The Right Profile signed a contract with Arista Records and was on its way.

It had been extraordinarily fun getting to this point. The Arista impresario Clive Davis had scouted the band at CBGB, the grimy New York club where bands like the Ramones and Talking Heads made their bones. Later, Davis invited the band to his swanky midtown office and put Aretha Franklin on the phone to chat up the boys about the upsides of Arista. Our budding rock star had more substantial career conversations with Springsteen himself, the fast-rising R.E.M., and other musical heroes. It was intoxicating to be so close to his childhood dream. And then he quit.

Somewhere along the way, he realized that as exhilarating as it was to get up onstage with a guitar and jump around like a maniac, the actual life of a rock star didn't appeal to him. From the outside, chasing fame and fortune seemed fantastic. But the more time he spent with people who had actually caught it, the more he knew that wasn't what he wanted. It meant living on the road, without much time for solitude; it meant living a life onstage. He realized he'd prefer to sit in a quiet room with a nice window and write stories, and then go home at night to a wife and kids. So that's what he set out to do.

This led him to graduate school and a few years of writing anything he could for whatever publication would have him. And then, as if beckoning from the heavens, came the *New York Times,* offering a dream job. For the son of a small-town newspaperman, this was ridiculously good fortune. For the first year at the *Times,* he pinched himself daily. One year gave way to five and then . . . he quit again. As exciting and rewarding as journalism could be, he realized he'd rather be off on his own, writing books—like this one.

The two of us have had more luck and more fun writing books together than we ever could have imagined.

Which naturally leads us to wonder: Should we take our own advice and think about quitting? After three *Freakonomics* books, can we possibly have more to say—and will anyone care? Maybe it's time for us to head over to the Experiments website and see what the coin has to say. If you never hear from us again, you'll know it came up heads . . .

. . .

Now that we've arrived at these last pages, it's pretty obvious: quitting is at the very core of thinking like a Freak. Or,
if that word still frightens you, let's think of it as "letting
go." Letting go of the conventional wisdoms that torment
us. Letting go of the artificial limits that hold us back—and
of the fear of admitting what we don't know. Letting go of
the habits of mind that tell us to kick into the corner of the
goal even though we stand a better chance by going up the
middle.

We might add that Winston Churchill, despite his famous advice to those Harrow schoolboys, was in fact one
of history's greatest quitters. Soon after entering politics he
quit one party for another, and later he quit government altogether. When he rejoined, he quit parties again. And when
he wasn't quitting, he was getting tossed out. He spent years
in the political wilderness, denouncing Britain's appease-
ment of the Nazis, and was returned to office only when that
policy's failure had led to total war. Even in the bleakest
moments, Churchill did not back down one inch from Hitler; he became "the greatest of all Britain's war leaders," as
the historian John Keegan put it. Perhaps it was that long
streak of quitting that helped Churchill build the fortitude
to tough it out when it was truly necessary. By now, he knew
what was worth letting go, and what was not.

. . .

All right, then: we've had our say. As you've seen, there are no magic bullets. All we've done is encourage you to think a bit differently, a bit harder, a bit more freely. Now it's your turn! We of course hope you enjoyed this book. But our greatest satisfaction would be if it helps you, even in some small measure, to go out and right some wrong, to ease some burden, or even—if this is your thing—to eat more hot dogs. Good luck, and let us know what you come up with.* Having made it this far, you too are now a Freak. So we are all in this together.

---

* Drop us a line at ThinkLikeAFreak@freakonomics.com.

Acknowledgments

Our biggest thanks, as always, go to the amazing people who let us tell their stories in this book and who opened their doors, memories, even their ledgers.

As ever, Suzanne Gluck is our North Star and Henry Ferris has been just the right man for the job. Thanks a million to both of you, and everyone at WME and William Morrow. Also to Alexis Kirschbaum and all the other very good people at Penguin U.K., present and past.

Jonathan Rosen lent another pair of eyes—exceedingly perceptive ones—when they were desperately needed.

Bourree Lam was tireless in research and all-around assistance; Laura L. Griffin was a most excellent fact-checker.

Hey, Harry Walker Agency: you are the greatest!

Special thanks to Erin Robertson and everyone at the Becker Center and the Greatest Good; also to the talented Freakonomics

Radio crew: Chris Bannon, Collin Campbell, Gretta Cohn, Andrew Gartrell, Ryan Hagen, David Herman, Diana Huynh, Suzie Lechtenberg, Jeff Mosenkis, Chris Neary, Greg Rosalsky, Molly Webster, Katherine Wells, and everyone else at WNYC.

From SDL: To the people closest to me, thank you for everything; you are better than I deserve.

From SJD: To Anya Dubner and Solomon Dubner and Ellen Dubner: you provide comfort and joy, pirouettes and nutmegs, explosions of love, all the days of my life.

Notes

Below you will find the source material for the stories we've told in this book. We are grateful, and indebted, to the many scholars, writers, and others whose research we relied upon. Let's also raise a glass to Wikipedia. It has improved immeasurably over the years that we have been writing books; it is extraordinarily valuable as a first stop to discover primary sources on nearly any topic. Thanks to all those who have contributed to it intellectually, financially, or otherwise.

CHAPTER 1: WHAT DOES IT MEAN TO THINK LIKE A FREAK?

1 **"IS A COLLEGE DEGREE STILL 'WORTH IT'"?**: See Stephen J. Dubner, "Freakonomics Goes to College, Parts 1 and 2," Freakonomics Radio, July 30, 2012, and August 16, 2012. As for the value of college and the returns on investment, the economist David Card has written widely and well on this topic. See also Ronald G. Ehrenberg, "American Higher

Education in Transition," *Journal of Economic Perspectives* 26, no. 1 (Winter 2012). / 1 **"Is it a good idea to pass along a family business . . . ?":** See Stephen J. Dubner, "The Church of Scionology," Freakonomics Radio, August 3, 2011. Some of the relevant papers are: Marianne Bertrand and Antoinette Schoar, "The Role of Family in Family Firms," *Journal of Economic Perspectives* 20, no. 2 (Spring 2006); Vikas Mehrotra, Randall Morck, Jungwook Shim, and Yupana Wiwattanakantang, "Adoptive Expectations: Rising Sons in Japanese Family Firms," *Journal of Financial Economics* 108, no. 3 (June 2013); and Francisco Pérez-González, "Inherited Control and Firm Performance," *American Economic Review* 96, no. 5 (2006) / 1 **"Whatever happened to the carpal tunnel syndrome epidemic?":** See Stephen J. Dubner, "Whatever Happened to the Carpal Tunnel Epidemic?," Freakonomics Radio, September 12, 2013. Drawn from research by Bradley Evanoff, an M.D. who studies occupational medicine at Washington University; among his relevant papers: T. Armstrong, A. M. Dale, A. Franzblau, and Evanoff, "Risk Factors for Carpal Tunnel Syndrome and Median Neuropathy in a Working Population," *Journal of Occupational and Environmental Medicine* 50, no. 12 (December 2008).

3 **IMAGINE YOU ARE A SOCCER PLAYER:** The statistics in this section were drawn from: Pierre-André Chiappori, Steven D. Levitt, Timothy Groseclose, "Testing Mixed-Strategy Equilibria When Players Are Heterogeneous: The Case of Penalty Kicks in Soccer," *The American Economic Review* 92, no. 4 (September 2002); see also Stephen J. Dubner and Steven D. Levitt, "How to Take Penalties: Freakonomics Explains," *The (U.K.) Times*, June 12, 2010. For the speed of soccer ball, see Eleftherios Kellis and Athanasios Katis, "Biomechanical Characteristics and Determinants of Instep Soccer Kick," *Journal of Sports Science and Medicine* 6

(2007). Thanks to Solomon Dubner for his insights into this passage, and for his great interest in footy.

9   **"IF YOU'RE GRUMPY, WHO THE HELL WANTS TO MARRY YOU?":** Spoken by the irrepressible and inimitable Justin Wolfers in Stephen J. Dubner, "Why Marry, Part 1," Freakonomics Radio, February 13, 2014. See: Betsey Stevenson and Wolfers, "Marriage and Divorce: Changes and Their Driving Forces," NBER working paper 12944 (March 2007); Alois Stutzer and Bruno S. Frey, "Does Marriage Make People Happy, or Do Happy People Get Married?," IZA discussion paper (October 2005).

10   **EVEN THE SMARTEST PEOPLE TEND TO SEEK OUT INFORMATION THAT CONFIRMS WHAT THEY ALREADY THINK:** See Stephen J. Dubner, "The Truth Is Out There . . . Isn't It?," Freakonomics Radio, November 23, 2011; drawn from research conducted by, among others, the Cultural Cognition Project. / 10 **It's also tempting to run with a herd:** See Stephen J. Dubner, "Riding the Herd Mentality," Freakonomics Radio, June 21, 2012.

11   **"FEW PEOPLE THINK MORE THAN TWO OR THREE TIMES A YEAR":** Like many historical quotes, this one is hard to verify for certain, but Shaw was at least famous during his lifetime for having said this. In 1933, *Reader's Digest* attributed the quote to Shaw, as did many other publications. Hat tip to Garson O'Toole of QuoteInvestigator.com, who provided considerable help in tracing this quote.

11   **CHILD CAR SEATS ARE A WASTE OF TIME:** See Joseph J. Doyle Jr. and Steven D. Levitt, "Evaluating the Effectiveness of Child Safety Seats and Seat Belts in Protecting Children From Injury," *Economic Inquiry* 48, no. 3 (July 2010); Stephen J. Dubner and Levitt, "The Seat-Belt Solution," *The New York Times Magazine,* July 10, 2005; Lev-

itt and Dubner, *SuperFreakonomics* (William Morrow, 2009). / 11 **The local-food movement can actually hurt the environment:** See Christopher L. Weber and H. Scott Matthews, "Food-Miles and the Relative Climate Impacts of Food Choices in the United States," *Environmental Science & Technology* 42, no. 10 (April 2008); and Stephen J. Dubner, "You Eat What You Are, Part 2," Freakonomics Radio, June 7, 2012.

11   OUR DISASTROUS MEETING WITH DAVID CAMERON: Thanks to Rohan Silva for the invitation to this and subsequent meetings (though never again with Mr. Cameron himself!) and to David Halpern and his Behavioral Insights Team. / 14 **"The closest thing the English have to a religion":** See Nigel Lawson, *The View from No. 11: Memoirs of a Tory Radical* (Bantam Press, 1992) / 14 **U.K. health-care costs:** See Adam Jurd, "Expenditure on Healthcare in the UK, 1997–2010," Office for National Statistics, May 2, 2012 / 14 **David Cameron biographical details:** We are especially indebted to Francis Elliott and James Hanning's *Cameron: Practically a Conservative* (Fourth Estate, 2012), originally published as *Cameron: The Rise of the New Conservative*, a thorough if somewhat tabloidy biography. / 16 **A massive share of the costs go to the final months:** for an interesting discussion of end-of-life medical care, see Ezekiel J. Emanuel, "Better, if Not Cheaper, Care," *New York Times*, January 4, 2013.

CHAPTER 2: THE THREE HARDEST WORDS IN THE ENGLISH LANGUAGE

19   A LITTLE GIRL NAMED MARY: Special thanks to Amanda Waterman, a developmental psychologist at the University of Leeds. There is a small but interesting literature on the topic of unanswerable questions, among both children and

adults, to which Waterman is an important contributor. See Waterman and Mark Blades, "Helping Children Correctly Say 'I Don't Know' to Unanswerable Questions," *Journal of Experimental Psychology: Applied* 17, no. 4 (2011); Waterman, Blades, and Christopher Spencer, "Interviewing Children and Adults: The Effect of Question Format on the Tendency to Speculate," *Applied Cognitive Psychology* 15 (2001); Waterman and Blades, "The Effect of Delay and Individual Differences on Children's Tendency to Guess," *Developmental Psychology* 49, no. 2 (February 2013); Alan Scoboria, Giuliana Mazzoni, and Irving Kirsch, " 'Don't Know' Responding to Answerable and Unanswerable Questions During Misleading and Hypnotic Interviews," *Journal of Experimental Psychology: Applied* 14, no. 3. (September 2008); Claudia M. Roebers and Olivia Fernandez, "The Effects of Accuracy Motivation and Children's and Adults' Event Recall, Suggestibility, and Their Answers to Unanswerable Questions," *Journal of Cognition and Development* 3, no. 4 (2002).

20 **"EVERYONE'S ENTITLED TO THEIR OWN OPINION BUT NOT TO THEIR OWN FACTS"**: Moynihan said this at a Jerome Levy Economics Institute Conference at the National Press Club in Washington, D.C., on October 26, 1995. According to *The Dictionary of Modern Proverbs* (Yale University Press, 2012) by Charles Clay Doyle, Wolfgang Mieder, and Fred R. Shapiro, the phrase was first said by Bernard M. Baruch.

21 **BELIEF IN THE DEVIL AND "ENTREPRENEURS OF ERROR"**: Thanks to Ed Glaeser for making this point in a lecture given at an April 2006 conference at the University Chicago in honor of Gary Becker. Devil poll numbers are from European Values Study 1990: Integrated Dataset (EVS, 2011), GESIS Data Archive, Cologne. 9/11 numbers are from a Gallup poll: "Blame for Sept. 11 Attacks Unclear for Many in

Islamic World," March 1, 2002; see also Matthew A. Gentz-kow and Jesse M. Shapiro, "Media, Education and Anti-Americanism in the Muslim World," *Journal of Economic Perspectives* 18, no. 3 (Summer 2004).

23　**THE FOLLY OF PREDICTION:** "Prediction is very difficult . . .": Niels Bohr was "fond of quoting" this line; it is strongly associated with a fellow Dane, the prominent cartoonist Storm P., although he is likely not the originator either. / 23 **One of the most impressive studies:** See Philip E. Tetlock, *Expert Political Judgment: How Good Is It? How Can We Know?* (Princeton University Press, 2005); and Stephen J. Dubner, "The Folly of Prediction," Freakonomics Radio, September 14, 2011. For economic predictions, see Jerker Denrell and Christina Fang, "Predicting the Next Big Thing: Success as a Signal of Poor Judgment," *Management Science* 56, no. 10 (2010); for NFL predictions, see Christopher Avery and Judith Chevalier, "Identifying Investor Sentiment From Price Paths: The Case of Football Betting," *Journal of Business* 72, no. 4 (1999). / 24 **A similar study by a firm called CXO Advisory Group:** See "Guru Grades," CXO Advisory Group / 25 **Smart people love to make smart-sounding predictions:** See Paul Krugman, "Why Most Economists' Predictions Are Wrong," *Red Herring*, June 1998. (Thanks to the Internet Archive Wayback Machine.) / 26 **More than the GDP of all but eighteen countries:** market caps of Google, Amazon, Facebook, and Apple are based on stock prices as of February 11, 2014; the eighteen countries are: Australia, Brazil, Canada, China, France, Germany, India, Indonesia, Italy, Japan, Mexico, Russia, South Korea, Spain, the Netherlands, the U.K., the U.S., and Turkey (see CIA World Factbook).

27　**WE DON'T EVEN KNOW OURSELVES ALL THAT WELL:** See Clayton R. Critcher and David Dunning, "How Chronic Self-

Views Influence (and Mislead) Self-Assessments of Task Performance: Self-Views Shape Bottom-Up Experiences with the Task," *Journal of Personality and Social Psychology* 97, no. 6 (2009). (Thanks to Danny Kahneman and Tom Gilovich for leading us to this paper.) See also: Dunning et al., "Why People Fail to Recognize Their Own Incompetence," *Current Directions in Psychological Science* 12, no. 3 (June 2003).

27 **WHEN ASKED TO RATE THEIR DRIVING SKILLS:** See Iain A. McCormick, Frank H. Walkey, and Dianne E. Green, "Comparative Perceptions of Driver Ability—A Confirmation and Expansion," *Accident Analysis & Prevention* 18, no. 3 (June 1986); and Ola Svenson, "Are We All Less Risky and More Skillful Than Our Fellow Drivers?," *Acta Psychologica* 47 (1981).

27 **"ULTRACREPIDARIANISM":** We are grateful to the continuing research by Anders Ericsson and his many colleagues, much of whose research is collected in Ericsson, Neil Charness, Paul J. Feltovich, and Robert R. Hoffman, *The Cambridge Handbook of Expertise and Expert Performance* (Cambridge University Press, 2006); see also Steven D. Levitt, John A. List, and Sally E. Sadoff, "Checkmate: Exploring Backward Induction Among Chess Players," *American Economics Review* 101, no. 2 (April 2011); Chris Argyris, "Teaching Smart People How to Learn," *Harvard Business Review*, May 1991. Our definition of "ultracrepidarianism" is from FreeDictionary.com.

28 **COSTS OF THE IRAQ WAR:** See Linda J. Bilmes, "The Financial Legacy of Iraq and Afghanistan: How Wartime Spending Decisions Will Constrain Future National Security Budgets," Harvard Kennedy School Faculty Research Working Paper Series RWP13-006 (March 2013); Amy Belasco, "The Cost of Iraq, Afghanistan, and Other Global War on

Terror Operations Since 9/11," Congressional Research Service, March 29, 2011.

30 **AN ELDERLY CHRISTIAN RADIO PREACHER NAMED HAROLD CAMPING:** See Robert D. McFadden, "Harold Camping, Dogged Forecaster of the End of the World, Dies at 92," *New York Times*, December 17, 2013; Dan Amira, "A Conversation with Harold Camping, Prophesier of Judgment Day," Daily Intelligencer blog, *New York Magazine*, May 11, 2011; Harold Camping, "We Are Almost There!," Familyradio .com. (Thanks to the Internet Archive Wayback Machine.)

30 **ROMANIAN WITCHES:** See Stephen J. Dubner, "The Folly of Prediction," Freakonomics Radio, September 14, 2011; "Witches Threaten Romanian Taxman After New Labor Law," BBC, January 6, 2011; Alison Mutler, "Romania's Witches May Be Fined If Predictions Don't Come True," Associated Press, February 8, 2011.

32 **SHIP'S COMPASSES AND METAL INTERFERENCE:** See A. R. T. Jonkers, *Earth's Magnetism in the Age of Sail* (Johns Hopkins University Press, 2003); T. A. Lyons, *A Treatise on Electromagnetic Phenomena and on the Compass and Its Deviations Aboard Ship, Vol. 2* (John Wiley & Sons, 1903). Thanks to Jonathan Rosen for pointing out this idea.

32 **CONSIDER A PROBLEM LIKE SUICIDE:** For a fuller treatment of this topic, see Stephen J. Dubner, "The Suicide Paradox," Freakonomics Radio, August 31, 2011. We are particularly indebted to the broad and deep research of David Lester, as well as multiple interviews with him. We also relied heavily on David M. Cutler, Edward L. Glaeser, and Karen E. Norberg, "Explaining the Rise in Youth Suicide," from Jonathan Gruber (editor), *Risky Behavior Among Youths: An Economic Analysis* (University of Chicago Press, 2001). Various reports from the Centers for Disease Control and

Prevention and the National Vital Statistics System were very helpful; see also Robert E. McKeown, Steven P. Cuffe, and Richard M. Schulz, "U.S. Suicide Rates by Age Group, 1970–2002: An Examination of Recent Trends," *American Journal of Public Health* 96, no. 10 (October 2006). On the topic of the "suicide paradox"—i.e., the link between suicide and increased well-being—see Cutler et al. as well as: A. F. Henry and J. F. Short, *Suicide and Homicide* (Free Press, 1954); David Lester, "Suicide, Homicide, and the Quality of Life: An Archival Study," *Suicide and Life-Threatening Behavior*, 1693 (fall 1986); Lester, "Suicide, Homicide, and the Quality of Life in Various Countries," *Acta Psychiatrica Scandinavica* 81 (1990); E. Hem et al., "Suicide Rates According to Education with a Particular Focus on Physicians in Norway 1960–2000," *Psychological Medicine* 35, no. 6 (June 2005); Mary C. Daly, Andrew J. Oswald, Daniel Wilson, Stephen Wu, "The Happiness-Suicide Paradox," Federal Reserve Bank of San Francisco working paper 2010–30; Daly, Wilson, and Norman J. Johnson, "Relative Status and Well-Being: Evidence from U.S. Suicide Deaths," Federal Reserve Bank of San Francisco working paper 2012–16. / 32 **The U.S. homicide rate is lower than it's been in fifty years:** See James Alan Fox and Marianne W. Zawitz, "Homicide Trends in the United States," Bureau of Justice Statistics; and "Crime in the United States 2012," Federal Bureau of Investigation's Uniform Crime Reports, Table 16. / 32 **The rate of traffic fatalities is at a historic low:** See Stephen J. Dubner, "The Most Dangerous Machine," Freakonomics Radio, December 5, 2013; Ian Savage, a Northwestern economist who studies transportation safety, was especially helpful in compiling this research. See also: "Traffic Safety Facts: 2012 Motor Vehicle Crashes: Overview," National Highway Traffic Safety Administration, November 2013.

40   IN TRYING TO MEASURE THE KNOCK-ON EFFECTS OF SENDING
     MILLIONS OF PEOPLE TO PRISON: See Steven D. Levitt, "The
     Effect of Prison Population Size on Crime Rates: Evidence
     from Prison Overcrowding Litigation," *The Quarterly Jour-*
     nal of Economics 111, no. 2 (May 1996) / 40 **In analyzing**
     the relationship between abortion and crime . . . : See
     John J. Donohue III and Levitt, "The Impact of Legalized
     Abortion on Crime," *The Quarterly Journal of Economics*
     116, no. 2 (May 2001).

41   A BETTER WAY TO GET GOOD FEEDBACK IS TO RUN A FIELD
     EXPERIMENT: One of the masters of modern field experimen-
     tation is John List, with whom we've collaborated a good
     bit, and whom we wrote about in Chapter 3 of *SuperFreak-*
     onomics. For an engaging tour of the topic, see Uri Gneezy
     and John A. List, *The Why Axis: Hidden Motives and the*
     Undiscovered Economics of Everyday Life (Public Affairs,
     2013).

42   DO EXPENSIVE WINES REALLY TASTE BETTER? For a fuller
     treatment of this topic, see Stephen J. Dubner, "Do More Ex-
     pensive Wines Taste Better?" Freakonomics Radio, Decem-
     ber 16, 2010. It includes the story of Steve Levitt's blind taste
     test at the Society of Fellows and Robin Goldstein's exten-
     sive blind-taste experiments. For the underlying research
     on Goldstein's findings, see Goldstein, Johan Almenberg,
     Anna Dreber, John W. Emerson, Alexis Herschkowitsch,
     and Jacob Katz, "Do More Expensive Wines Taste Better?
     Evidence from a Large Sample of Blind Tastings," *Journal*
     of Wine Economics 3, no. 1 (Spring 2008); see also Ste-
     ven D. Levitt, "Cheap Wine," Freakonomics.com, July 16,
     2008. While Goldstein's research suggests that wine ex-
     perts are far more discerning than average drinkers, there
     is further research that challenges even this assumption.

Another paper in *The Journal of Wine Economics* found experts' judgment to be—well, rather inexpert. One study of judges at wine competitions, for instance, found that most wines that win a gold medal in one competition received no award at all in another. "Thus," wrote the author, "many wines that are viewed as extraordinarily good at some competitions are viewed as below average at others." See Robert T. Hodgson, "An Analysis of the Concordance Among 13 U.S. Wine Competitions," *Journal of Wine Economics* 4, no. 1 (spring 2009). / 45 **Osteria L'Intrepido's terrible wine list:** Goldstein revealed his *Wine Spectator* Award of Excellence prank at the American Association of Wine Economists' 2008 annual conference. The incident received widespread media coverage. *Wine Spectator* vigorously defended its award system; the executive editor said the magazine never claimed to visit every restaurant that applied for an award, and that it did its due diligence on Osteria L'Intrepido—looking over its website and calling the restaurant—but that it kept reaching an answering machine. See also: Goldstein, "What Does It Take to Get a Wine Spectator Award of Excellence," Blindtaste.com, August 15, 2008.

47 **REMEMBER THOSE BRITISH SCHOOLCHILDREN:** See Amanda H. Waterman and Mark Blades, "Helping Children Correctly Say 'I Don't Know' to Unanswerable Questions, *Journal of Experimental Psychology: Applied* 17, no. 4 (2011).

CHAPTER 3: WHAT'S YOUR PROBLEM?

50 **TEACHER SKILL:** See the two-part National Bureau of Economic Research paper by Raj Chetty, John N. Friedman,

and Jonah E. Rockoff, "The Long-term Impacts of Teachers: Teach Value-added and Student Outcomes in Adulthood" (September 2013) / 50 **Smart women now have so many more job options:** See Marigee P. Bacolod, "Do Alternative Opportunities Matter? The Role of Female Labor Markets in the Decline of Teacher Supply and Teacher Quality, 1940–1990," *Review of Economics and Statistics* 89, no. 4 (November 2007); and Harold O. Levy, "Why the Best Don't Teach," *The New York Times,* September 9, 2000. / 50 **Finnish teachers (e.g.) vs. American teachers:** See "Top Performing Countries," Center on International Education Benchmarking (2013), available at http://www.ncee.org; Byron Auguste, Paul Kihn, and Matt Miller, "Closing the Talent Gap: Attracting and Retaining Top-Third Graduates to Careers in Teaching," McKinsey & Company (Sept 2010). (The McKinsey report has been criticized because it ranks the terciles by SAT score/high school GPA, and only surveys a small population of new teachers.) Thanks to Eric Kumbier for making this point to us in an e-mail. / 50 **Parental influence on kids' education:** See, inter alia, Marianne Bertrand and Jessica Pan, "The Trouble with Boys: Social Influences and the Gender Gap in Disruptive Behavior," *American Economic Journal: Applied Economics* 5, no. 1 (2013); Shannon M. Pruden, Susan C. Levine, and Janellen Huttenlocher, "Children's Spatial Thinking: Does Talk About the Spatial World Matter?," *Developmental Science* 14 (November 2011); Bruce Sacerdote, "How Large Are the Effects from Changes in Family Environment? A Study of Korean American Adoptees," *The Quarterly Journal of Economics* 122, no.1 (2007); Roland G. Fryer Jr. and Steven D. Levitt, "Understanding the Black-White Test Score Gap in the First Two Years of School," *The Review of Economics and Statistics* 86, no. 2 (May 2004); Huttenlocher, Marina Vasilyeva, Elina Cymerman, and Susan Levine, "Language

Input and Child Syntax," *Cognitive Psychology* 45, no. 3 (2002). / 51 **"Why do American kids know less . . . ?":** See 2012 report from Program for International Student Assessment (PISA) / 51 **Turn that child over . . . so the teachers can work their magic:** for a rare example of a spirited argument in this vein, see "The Depressing Data on Early Childhood Investment," interview with Jerome Kagan by Paul Solman, PBS.org (March 7, 2013).

52 **THE LEGEND OF TAKERU KOBAYASHI:** We are grateful to Kobi for the many hours of fascinating conversation stretching over what turned out to be several years, and to all those who helped facilitate those conversations, including Maggie James, Noriko Okubo, Akiko Funatsu, Anna Berry, Kumi, and others. Kobi is so convinced that competitive eating is an acquired skill that he says he could train one of us to eat fifty HDB with just six months of training. We have yet to take him up on this offer. Dubner did, however, get one lesson from Kobi, at Gray's Papaya in New York:

We are indebted to the many journalists who have written about Kobi and the sport of competitive eating, especially Jason Fagone, the author of *Horsemen of the Esophagus: Competitive Eating and the Big Fat American Dream* (Crown, 2006). Fagone steered us in the right direction at the outset. We also drew upon: Fagone, "Dog Bites Man," Slate.com, July 8, 2010; Bill Belew, "Takeru 'Tsunami' Kobayashi Training & Techniques to Defeat Joey Chestnut," The Biz of Knowledge website, June 29, 2007; "How Do You Speed Eat?" BBC News Magazine, July 4, 2006; Sarah Goldstein, "The Gagging and the Glory," Salon.com, April 19, 2006; Josh Ozersky, "On Your Mark. Get Set. Pig Out," *New York,* June 26, 2005; Chris Ballard, "That Is Going to Make You Money Someday," *The New York Times,* August 31, 2003; Associated Press, "Kobayashi's Speedy Gluttony Rattles Foes," ESPN.com, July 4, 2001. / 53 **Its promoters admit they concocted that history:** See Sam Roberts, "No, He Did Not Invent the Publicity Stunt," *New York Times,* August 18, 2010. / 55 **A schoolboy choked to death:** See Tama Miyake, "Fast Food," *Metropolis,* November 17, 2006. / 56 **The opponent was a half-ton Kodiak bear:** See Larry Getlen, "The Miracle That Is Kobayashi," *The Black Table* website, May 19, 2005. / 58 **The hot-dog-bun challenge:** Thanks to the Freakonomics Radio crew for trying this (and failing). As producer Greg Rosalsky put it: "The first bun soaks up your saliva like a sponge and then it seems virtually impossible to eat the second one." / 61 **"I wish there were hot dogs in jail":** See "Kobayashi Freed, Pleads Not Guilty," ESPN.com News Services (with reporting from the Associated Press), ESPN New York, July 5, 2010. / 63 **Even elite athletes can be tricked:** See M. R. Stone, K. Thomas, M. Wilkinson, A. M. Jones, A. St. Clair Gibson, and K. G. Thompson, "Effects of Deception on Exercise Performance: Implications for Determinants of Fatigue in Humans," *Medicine & Science in Sports & Exercise* 44, No. 3 (March 2012); Gina Kolata, "A Little Deception Helps Push Athletes to the Limit," *New York Times*, September 19, 2011. Thanks also to Kolata for the Roger Bannister quote, which we appropriated. / 64 **"I can keep going":** Thanks again to Jason Fagone for this quote; it appeared in the May 2006 issue of *The Atlantic,* in an excerpt from his *Horsemen of the Esophagus* book.

CHAPTER 4: LIKE A BAD DYE JOB, THE TRUTH IS IN THE ROOTS

66 **"STARVATION IS THE CHARACTERISTIC . . .":** See Amartya Sen, *Poverty and Famines: An Essay on Entitlement and Deprivation* (Oxford Univ. Press, 1981). / 67 **We throw away an astonishing 40 percent of the food:** See "USDA and EPA Launch U.S. Food Waste Challenge," USDA new release, June 4, 2013.

67 **THE RISE AND FALL IN VIOLENT CRIME:** See Steven D. Levitt and Stephen J. Dubner, *Freakonomics* (William Morrow, 2005); and Levitt, "Understanding Why Crime Fell in the 1990s: Four Factors That Explain the Decline and Six That Do Not," *Journal of Economic Perspectives* 18, no. 1 (winter 2004), pp. 163–190. / 68 **The homicide rate today . . . lower than it was in 1960:** See Erica L. Smith and Alexia Cooper, "Homicide in the U.S. Known to Law Enforcement, 2011," Bureau of Justice Statistics (Dec. 2013); U.S. Department of Justice, Federal Bureau of Investigation, "Crime in the United States, 2011," Table 1; Barry Krisberg, Carolina Guzman, Linh Vuong, "Crime and Economic Hard Times," National Council on Crime and Delinquency (February 2009); and James Alan Fox and Marianne W. Zawitz, "Homicide Trends in the United States," Bureau of Justice

Statistics (2007). / 69 **The abortion-crime link:** See Levitt and Dubner, *Freakonomics* (William Morrow, 2005); and John J. Donohue III and Levitt, "The Impact of Legalized Abortion on Crime," *The Quarterly Journal of Economics* 116, no. 2 (May 2001).

70   LET'S PRETEND YOU ARE A GERMAN FACTORY WORKER: See Jörg Spenkuch, "The Protestant Ethic and Work: Micro Evidence From Contemporary Germany," University of Chicago working paper. Also based on author interviews with Spenkuch, and we are grateful to Spenkuch for his comments on our manuscript. For further recent evidence of the Protestant work ethic, see Andre van Hoorn, Robbert Maseland, "Does a Protestant Work Ethic Exist? Evidence from the Well-Being Effect of Unemployment," *Journal of Economic Behavior & Organization* 91 (July 2013). Meanwhile, Davide Cantoni has argued that the Protestant ethic did not improve economic outcomes in Germany; see Cantoni, "The Economic Effects of the Protestant Reformation: Testing the Weber Hypothesis in the German Lands," job market paper, November 10, 2009. / 73 **In defense, however, of German Catholicism . . . (footnote):** See Spenkuch and Philipp Tillmann, "Elite Influence? Religion, Economics, and the Rise of the Nazis," working paper, 2013.

73   WHY, FOR INSTANCE, ARE SOME ITALIAN TOWNS . . . : See Luigi Guiso, Paola Sapienza, and Luigi Zingales, "Long-Term Persistence," July 2013 working paper; see also earlier versions by same authors: "Long-Term Cultural Persistence," September 2012 working paper; and "Long-Term Persistence," European University Institute working paper 2008. Hat tip to Hans-Joachim Voth and Nico Voigtländer, "Hatred Transformed: How Germans Changed Their Minds About Jews, 1890–2006," *Vox,* May 1, 2012.

74 **ETHNIC STRIFE IN AFRICA**: See Stelios Michalopoulos and Elias Papaioannou, "The Long-Run Effects of the Scramble for Africa," NBER working paper, November 2011; and Elliott Green, "On the Size and Shape of African States," *International Studies Quarterly* 56, no. 2 (June 2012).

74 **THE SCARS OF COLONIALISM STILL HAUNT SOUTH AMERICA AS WELL**: See Melissa Dell, "The Persistent Effects of Peru's Mining *Mita*," MIT working paper, January 2010; and Daron Acemoglu, Camilo Garcia-Jimeno, and James A. Robinson, "Finding Eldorado: Slavery and Long-Run Development in Colombia," NBER working paper, June 2012.

75 **THE SALT-SENSITIVITY THEORY OF AFRICAN-AMERICAN HYPERTENSION**: This section is based on author interview with Roland Fryer as reflected in Stephen J. Dubner, "Toward a Unified Theory of Black America," *New York Times Magazine,* March 20, 2005. We are also grateful for the excellent article by Mark Warren in *Esquire,* "Roland Fryer's Big Ideas" (December 2005). See also: David M. Cutler, Roland G. Fryer Jr., and Edward L. Glaeser, "Racial Differences in Life Expectancy: The Impact of Salt, Slavery, and Selection," unpublished manuscript, Harvard University and NBER, March 1, 2005; and Katherine M. Barghaus, David M. Cutler, Roland G. Fryer Jr., and Edward L. Glaeser, "An Empirical Examination of Racial Differences in Health," unpublished manuscript, Harvard University, University of Pennsylvania, and NBER, November 2008. For further background, see: Gary Taubes, "Salt, We Misjudged You," *The New York Times,* June 3, 2012; Nicholas Bakalar, "Patterns: Less Salt Isn't Always Better for the Heart," *The New York Times,* November 29, 2011; Martin J. O'Donnell et al., "Urinary Sodium and Potassium Excretion and Risk of Cardiovascular Events," *The Journal of the American Med-*

ical Association 306, no. 20 (November 23/30, 2011); Michael H. Alderman, "Evidence Relating Dietary Sodium to Cardiovascular Disease," *Journal of the American College of Nutrition* 25, no. 3 (2006); Jay Kaufman, "The Anatomy of a Medical Myth," *Is Race "Real"?*, SSRC Web Forum June 7, 2006; Joseph E. Inikori and Stanley L. Engerman, *The Atlantic Slave Trade: Effects on Economies, Societies and Peoples in Africa, the Americas, and Europe* (Duke University Press, 1998); and F. C. Luft et al., "Salt Sensitivity and Resistance of Blood Pressure. Age and Race as Factors in Physiological Responses," *Hypertension* 17 (1991). / 75 **"An Englishman Tastes the Sweat of an African":** Courtesy of the John Carter Brown Library at Brown University. Original source: M. Chambon, *Le Commerce de l'Amerique par Marseille* (Avignon, 1764), vol. 2, plate XI, facing p. 400.

78 **"WE LIVE IN AN AGE OF SCIENCE . . .":** See Roy Porter, *The Greatest Benefit to Mankind: A Medical History of Humanity from Antiquity to the Present* (HarperCollins, 1997).

78 **CONSIDER THE ULCER:** The story of Barry Marshall (and Robin Warren) is fascinating and heroic from start to end. We strongly encourage you to read more about him, in any or all of the following works cited, which also include more general information about ulcers and the pharmaceutical industry. For the story of Marshall himself, we were most reliant on a wonderful long interview conducted by the estimable Norman Swan, an Australian physician who works as a journalist. See Norman Swan, "Interviews with Australian Scientists: Professor Barry Marshall," Australian Academy of Science, 2008. Thanks to Dr. Marshall himself for offering his useful comments on what we wrote about him here and in Chapter 5. We are also indebted to: Kathryn Schulz, "Stress Doesn't Cause Ulcers! Or, How to Win a Nobel Prize in One Easy Lesson: Barry Marshall on

Being . . . Right," Slate.com, September 9, 2010; Pamela Weintraub, "The Dr. Who Drank Infectious Broth, Gave Himself an Ulcer, and Solved a Medical Mystery," *Discover,* March 2010; and "Barry J. Marshall, Autobiography," The Nobel Prize in Physiology or Medicine 2005, Nobelprize .org, 2005. / 79 **The first true blockbuster drugs:** See Melody Petersen, *Our Daily Meds: How the Pharmaceutical Companies Transformed Themselves into Slick Marketing Machines and Hooked the Nation on Prescription Drugs* (Sarah Crichton Books, 2008); and Shannon Brownlee, "Big Pharma's Golden Eggs," *Washington Post,* April 6, 2008; "Having an Ulcer Is Getting a Lot Cheaper," *BusinessWeek,* May 8, 1994. / 79 **In the past, some medical researcher might have suggested . . . :** In particular we are thinking of Dr. A. Stone Freedberg of Harvard, who in 1940 published a paper "identifying similar bacteria in 40 percent of patients with ulcers and stomach cancer"; see Lawrence K. Altman, "Two Win Nobel Prize for Discovering Bacterium Tied to Stomach Ailments," *The New York Times,* October 4, 2005; and Lawrence K. Altman, "A Scientist, Gazing Toward Stockholm, Ponders 'What If?,'" *New York Times,* December 6, 2005. / 82 **Even today, many people still believe that ulcers are caused by stress . . . :** Perhaps they are still swayed by New York City's famously feisty mayor Ed Koch. "I'm the sort of person who will never get ulcers," he once said. "Why? Because I say exactly what I think. I'm the sort of person who might give other people ulcers." See Maurice Carroll, "How's He Doing? How's He Doing?," *New York Times,* December 24, 1978.

85 **THE POWER OF POOP:** This section was based primarily on author interviews with the gastroenterologists Thomas Borody, Alexander Khoruts, and Michael Levitt (father of Steve Levitt), as reflected in Stephen J. Dubner, "The Power of Poop," Freakonomics Radio, March 4, 2011. We

are also grateful to Borody for offering useful comments to this section. See also: Borody, Sudarshan Paramsothy, and Gaurav Agrawal, "Fecal Microbiota Transplantation: Indications, Methods, Evidence, and Future Directions," *Current Gastroenterology Reports* 15, no. 337 (July 2013); W. H. Wilson Tang et al., "Intestinal Microbial Metabolism of Phosphatidylcholine and Cardiovascular Risk," *New England Journal of Medicine* 368, no. 17 (April 2013); Olga C. Aroniadis and Lawrence J. Brandt, "Fecal Microbiota Transplantation: Past, Present and Future," *Current Opinion in Gastroenterology* 29, no. 1 (January 2013); "Jonathan Eisen: Meet Your Microbes," TEDMED Talk, Washington, D.C., April 2012; Borody and Khoruts, "Fecal Microbiota Transplantation and Emerging Applications," *Nature Reviews Gastroenterology & Hepatology* 9, no. 2 (2011); Khoruts et al., "Changes in the Composition of the Human Fecal Microbiome After Bacteriotherapy for Recurrent *Clostridium Difficile*–Associated Diarrhea," *Journal of Clinical Gastroenterology* 44, no. 5 (May/June 2010); Borody et al., "Bacteriotherapy Using Fecal Flora: Toying with Human Motions," *Journal of Clinical Gastroenterology* 38, no. 6 (July 2004). / 85 **Looks like chocolate milk:** That is according to Josbert Keller, a gastroenterologist at the HagaZiekenhuis hospital in the Hague, an author of "Duodenal Infusion of Donor Feces for Recurrent *Clostridium difficile*," *New England Journal of Medicine* 368 (2013):407–415; see also Denise Grady, "When Pills Fail, This, er, Option Provides a Cure," *New York Times,* January 16, 2013. / 85 **Colitis "previously an incurable disease":** See Borody and Jordana Campbell, "Fecal Microbiota Transplantation: Techniques, Applications, and Issues," *Gastroenterology Clinics of North America* 41 (2012); and Borody, Eloise F. Warren, Sharyn Leis, Rosa Surace, and Ori Ashman, "Treatment of Ulcerative Colitis Using Fecal

Bacteriotherapy," *Journal of Clinical Gastroenterology* 37, no. 1 (July 2003).

CHAPTER 5: THINK LIKE A CHILD

88 **"SOPHISTICATION" AND THE SOPHISTS (FOOTNOTE):** Drawn from the "Sophisticated" entry on worldwidewords.org, by the excellent British etymologist Michael Quinion.

89 **"TO EXPLAIN ALL NATURE IS TOO DIFFICULT A TASK . . .":** See Isaac Newton and J. E. McGuire, "Newton's 'Principles of Philosophy': An Intended Preface for the 1704 'Opticks' and a Related Draft Fragment," *The British Journal for the History of Science* 5, no. 2 (December 1970); hat tip to Freakonomics Radio producer Katherine Wells, who scripted this for Stephen J. Dubner, "The Truth Is Out There . . . Isn't It?," Freakonomics Radio, November 23, 2011.

90 **DRUNK WALKING:** See Steven D. Levitt and Stephen J. Dubner, *SuperFreakonomics* (William Morrow, 2009) / 90 **Mom-and-pop bagel-delivery outfit:** Levitt and Dubner, *Freakonomics* (William Morrow, 2005) / 91 **Guns versus swimming pools:** Levitt and Dubner, *Freakonomics*.

91 **POOR VISION AND CLASSROOM PERFORMANCE:** See Stephen J. Dubner, "Smarter Kids at 10 Bucks a Pop," Freakonomics Radio, April 8, 2011. This report was based primarily on author interviews with Paul Glewwe and Albert Park and drew on their paper "Visualizing Development: Eyeglasses and Academic Performance in Rural Primary Schools in China," University of Minnesota Center for International Food and Agricultural Policy, working paper WP12-2 (2012), co-authored with Meng Zhao. See also: Douglas Heingartner, "Better Vision for the World, on a Budget," *New York Times,*

January 2, 2010; and "Comprehensive Eye Exams Particularly Important for Classroom Success," American Optometric Association (2008). For the "four-eyes" stigma and "planos" (in footnote), see Dubner, "Playing the Nerd Card," Freakonomics Radio, May 31, 2012.

93 **AS ALBERT EINSTEIN LIKED TO SAY** . . . : Thanks again to Garson O'Toole at QuoteInvestigator.com.

94 **LET'S RETURN BRIEFLY TO BARRY MARSHALL:** Once again, we drew heavily from the excellent interview of Marshall conducted by Norman Swan, "Interviews with Australian Scientists: Professor Barry Marshall," Australian Academy of Science, 2008.

96 **EXPERT PERFORMANCE:** See, for starters, Stephen J. Dubner and Steven D. Levitt, "A Star Is Made," *The New York Times Magazine,* May 7, 2006. Our enduring thanks to K. Anders Ericsson; his work and that of his many fascinating colleagues is well represented in Ericsson, Neil Charness, Paul J. Feltovich, and Robert R. Hoffman, *The Cambridge Handbook of Expertise and Expert Performance* (Cambridge University Press, 2006). For related books on the topic, see Daniel Coyle, *The Talent Code* (Bantam, 2009); Geoff Colvin, *Talent Is Overrated* (Portfolio, 2008); and Malcolm Gladwell, *Outliers* (Little, Brown & Co., 2008).

98 **PRIZE-LINKED SAVINGS:** For a fuller treatment of this topic, see Stephen J. Dubner, "Could a Lottery Be the Answer to America's Poor Savings Rate?," Freakonomics Radio, November 18, 2010; and Dubner, "Who Could Say No to a 'No-Lose Lottery?,'" Freakonomics Radio, Dec. 2, 2010. These episodes featured interviews with, among many others, Melissa S. Kearney and Peter Tufano, both of whom are extremely knowledgeable about the topic. See, e.g., Kearney, Tufano, Jonathan Guryan, and Erik Hurst, "Making Savers

Winners: An Overview of Prize-Linked Saving Products," in Olivia S. Mitchell and Annamaria Lusardi (eds.), *Financial Literacy: Implications for Retirement Security and the Financial Marketplace* (Oxford University Press, 2011).

101 **KIDS ARE HARDER TO FOOL WITH MAGIC:** The Alex Stone section was based primarily on author interviews. See also *Fooling Houdini: Magicians, Mentalists, Math Geeks, and the Hidden Powers of the Mind* (HarperCollins, 2012); and Steven D. Levitt, "*Fooling Houdini* Author Alex Stone Answers Your Questions," Freakonomics.com, July 23, 2012. On the point of "paying attention," Stone acknowledges the insights of the developmental psychologist Alison Gopnik, author of *The Philosophical Baby: What Children's Minds Tell Us About Truth, Love, and the Meaning of Life* (Farrar, Straus and Giroux, 2009). For further reading on children and illusion, see Bruce Bower, "Adults Fooled by Visual Illusion, But Not Kids," *ScienceNews* via Wired.com, November 23, 2009; and Vincent H. Gaddis, "The Art of Honest Deception," StrangeMag.com.

104 **ISAAC BASHEVIS SINGER WRITING FOR KIDS:** See Singer, "Why I Write for Children," prepared for a 1970 award-acceptance speech, read at his 1978 Nobel acceptance speech, and reprinted in Singer, *Nobel Lecture* (Farrar, Straus & Giroux, 1979). Thanks to Jonathan Rosen for bringing this (along with many other good things) to our attention.

CHAPTER 6: LIKE GIVING CANDY TO A BABY

105 **AMANDA AND THE M&M'S:** A charming animated version of this story appears in *Freakonomics: The Movie*. Chad Troutwine was the lead producer of the film; the director

Seth Gordon headed up the team that created the Amanda section.

107 **THE AVERAGE U.S. ADULT WEIGHS ABOUT 25 POUNDS MORE TODAY THAN A FEW DECADES AGO:** See Centers for Disease Control, "Mean Body Weight, Height, and Body Mass Index, United States 1960–2002"; USDA, "Profiling Food Consumption in America," chapter 2 in the *Agriculture Factbook 2001-2002*; USDA "Percent of Household Final Consumption Expenditures Spent on Food, Alcoholic Beverages, and Tobacco That Were Consumed at Home, by Selected Countries, 2012," ERS Food Expenditure Series. / 107 **Why have we gotten so fat?:** There is a large and sometimes confusing literature on the relationship between food and price, with considerable dissent over the methodology of measuring food costs. Some researchers, for instance, take issue with the cost-per-calorie method. Two examples: Fred Kuchler and Hayden Stewart, "Price Trends Are Similar for Fruits, Vegetables, and Snack Foods," Report ERR-55, USDA Economic Research Service; and Andrea Carlson and Elizabeth Frazao, "Are Healthy Foods Really More Expensive? It Depends on How You Measure the Price," *USDA Economic Information Bulletin* 96 (May 2012). Among the research that most closely represents what we've written in this chapter, see: Michael Grossman, Erdal Tekin, and Roy Wada, "Food Prices and Body Fatness Among Youths," NBER working paper, June 2013; Stephen J. Dubner, "100 Ways to Fight Obesity," Freakonomics Radio, March 27, 2013; Pablo Monsivais and Adam Drewnowski, "The Rising Cost of Low-Energy-Density Foods," *Journal of the American Dietetic Association* 107, no. 12 (December 2007); Tara Parker-Pope, "A High Price for Healthy Food," *The New York Times* (Well blog), December 5, 2007; Cynthia L. Ogden, Cheryl D. Fryar, Margaret D. Carroll, and Katherine M. Flegal, "Mean Body Weight,

Height, and Body Mass Index, United States 1960–2002," *Advance Data from Vital and Health Statistics* 347 (National Center for Health Statistics, 2004); David M. Cutler, Edward L. Glaeser, and Jesse M. Shapiro, "Why Have Americans Become More Obese?" *Journal of Economic Perspectives* 17, no. 3 (Summer 2003).

108 **CONSIDER A 2011 TRAFFIC ACCIDENT:** See Josh Tapper, "Did Chinese Laws Keep Strangers from Helping Toddler Hit by Truck," *The (Toronto) Star,* October 18, 2011; Li Wenfang, "Hospital Offers Little Hope for Girl's Survival," *China Daily,* October 17, 2011; Michael Wines, "Bystanders' Neglect of Injured Toddler Sets Off Soul-Searching on Web Sites in China," *New York Times,* October 11, 2011. Thanks to Robert Alan Greevy for bringing this story to our attention.

109 **CASH FOR GRADES:** See Steven D. Levitt, John A. List, Susanne Neckermann, and Sally Sadoff, "The Impact of Short-Term Incentives on Student Performance," University of Chicago working paper, September 2011; and Roland G. Fryer Jr., "Financial Incentives and Student Achievement: Evidence from Randomized Trials," *The Quarterly Journal of Economics* 126, no. 4 (2011).

112 **ROBERT CIALDINI'S EXPERIMENTS WITH ELECTRICITY CONSUMPTION AND PETRIFIED-WOOD THEFT:** Drawn from author interviews with Cialdini as reflected in Stephen J. Dubner, "Riding the Herd Mentality," Freakonomics Radio, June 21, 2012. Cialdini's book *Influence* is a fantastic introduction to his way of thinking. See also: Jessica M. Nolan, P. Wesley Schultz, Robert B. Cialdini, Noah J. Goldstein, and Vladas Griskevicius, "Normative Social Influence Is Underdetected," *Personality and Social Psychology Bulletin* 34, no. 913 (2008); Goldstein, Cialdini, and Steve Martin, *Yes!: 50 Secrets from the Science of Persuasion* (Free Press,

2008); Schultz, Nolan, Cialdini, Goldstein, and Griskevicius, "The Constructive, Destructive, and Reconstructive Power of Social Norms," *Psychological Science* 18, no. 5 (2007); Cialdini, Linda J. Demaine, Brad J. Sagarin, Daniel W. Barrett, Kelton Rhoads, and Patricia L. Winter, "Managing Social Norms for Persuasive Impact," *Social Influence* 1, no. 1 (2006); Cialdini, "Crafting Normative Messages to Protect the Environment," *Current Directions in Psychological Science* 12 (2003). In the petrified-wood study, there were other sign options, including one that showed a park visitor stealing wood, accompanied by the message "Please don't remove petrified wood from the park." This sign did outperform the no-sign option.

117 **BRIAN MULLANEY, SMILE TRAIN, AND "ONCE-AND-DONE":** This section was drawn primarily from author interviews with Mullaney, an unpublished memoir by Mullaney, and the research reflected in Amee Kamdar, Steven D. Levitt, John A. List, and Chad Syverson, "Once and Done: Leveraging Behavioral Economics to Increase Charitable Contributions," University of Chicago working paper, 2013. See also: Stephen J. Dubner and Levitt, "Bottom-Line Philanthropy," *New York Times Magazine,* March 9, 2008; and James Andreoni, "Impure Altruism and Donations to Public Goods: A Theory of Warm-Glow Giving," *The Economic Journal* 100, no. 401 (June 1990). For another version of the "once-and-done" story, see Uri Gneezy and List, *The Why Axis: Hidden Motives and the Undiscovered Economics of Everyday Life* (Public Affairs, 2013). / 119 **Peter Buffett and "conscience laundering":** See Peter Buffett, "The Charitable-Industrial Complex," *New York Times,* July 26, 2013. For a related conversation with Buffett, on the topic of his having won "the ovarian lottery"—he is a son of Warren Buffett—see Dubner, "Growing Up Buffett," May 13, 2011.

127 **ENTER THE PING-PONG TEAMS:** See Henry A. Kissinger, *On China* (Penguin, 2011); "Ping-Pong Diplomacy (April 6–17, 1971)," *AmericanExperience.com*; David A. DeVoss, "Ping-Pong Diplomacy," *Smithsonian,* April 2002; "The Ping Heard Round the World," *Time,* April 26, 1971.

128 **ZAPPOS:** This section was based in part on author interviews with Tony Hsieh and a visit to Zappos headquarters. See also: Hsieh, *Delivering Happiness: A Path to Profits, Passion, and Purpose* (Business Plus, 2010); Hsieh, "How I Did It: Zappos's CEO on Going to Extremes for Customers," *Harvard Business Review,* July 2010; Robin Wauters, "Amazon Closes Zappos Deal, Ends Up Paying $1.2 Billion," *TechCrunch,* November 2, 2009; Hsieh, "Amazon Closing," Zappos.com, November 2, 2009; Alexandra Jacobs, "Happy Feet," *The New Yorker,* September 14, 2009. "You guys are just the best" testimonial on Zappos.com by Jodi M., February 21, 2006.

131 **MEXICO CITY HAS LONG SUFFERED FROM DREADFUL TRAFFIC JAMS:** See Lucas W. Davis, "The Effect of Driving Restrictions on Air Quality in Mexico City," *Journal of Political Economy* 116, no. 1 (2008); and Gunnar S. Eskeland and Tarhan Feyzioglu, "Rationing Can Backfire: The Day Without a Car in Mexico City," World Bank Policy Research Dept., December 1995.

131 **HFC-23 AND PAYING POLLUTERS TO POLLUTE:** "Phasing Out of HFC-23 Projects," *Verified Carbon Standard,* January 1, 2014; "Explosion of HFC-23 Super Greenhouse Gases Is Expected," Environmental Investigation Agency press release, June 24, 2013; EIA, "Two Billion Tonne Climate Bomb: How to Defuse the HFC-23 Problem," June 2013; "U.N. CDM Acts to Halt Flow of Millions of Suspect HFC-23 Carbon Credits"; Elisabeth Rosenthal and Andrew W. Lehren, "Profits on

Carbon Credits Drive Output of a Harmful Gas," *New York Times,* August 8, 2012.

133 **"THE COBRA EFFECT"**: See Stephen J. Dubner, "The Cobra Effect," Freakonomics Radio, October 11, 2012; Horst Siebert, *Der Kobra-Effekt: Wie man Irrwege der Wirtschaftspolitik vermeidet* (Deutsche Verlags-Anstalt, 2001); Sipho Kings, "Catch 60 Rats, Win a Phone," *Mail & Guardian* (South Africa), October 26, 2012. / 133 **As Mark Twain once wrote . . .** : See Mark Twain, *Mark Twain's Own Autobiography: The Chapters from the North American Review,* ed. Michael Kiskis (University of Wisconsin Press, 1990). We are grateful to Jared Morton for bringing this quote to our attention.

CHAPTER 7: WHAT DO KING SOLOMON AND DAVID LEE ROTH HAVE IN COMMON?

137 **KING SOLOMON**: The biblical quotes here are from *The Tanakh* (Jewish Publication Societies, 1917). The story of Solomon and the maternity dispute can be found beginning at 1 Kings 3:16. We also relied on Rabbi Joseph Telushkin, *Biblical Literacy* (William Morrow, 1997). There is a great deal of commentary surrounding this story, as there is with many biblical tales. For a good modern summary, which includes ancient commentary, see Mordecai Kornfeld, "King Solomon's Wisdom," *Rabbi Mordecai Kornfeld's Weekly Parasha-Page*; and Baruch C. Cohen, "The Brilliant Wisdom of King Solomon," *Jewish Law Commentary,* July 10, 1998. Both of these interpretations stress the incentives presented by *yibbum,* "a rite which must be performed when a man who has a living brother dies childless." The Solomon story has also been dissected by nonbiblical scholars, including the economists Avinash K. Dixit and Barry J.

Nalebuff in *The Art of Strategy* (Norton, 2008). Dixit and Nalebuff approach the story as a game-theory puzzle and conclude that the second woman erred in agreeing with King Solomon to divide the child in half. Indeed, why would the second woman go to the trouble to steal the baby and then so blithely agree to have it killed? Also, once the first woman renounced ownership, why wouldn't the second woman simply keep quiet and accept the baby? By this reckoning, Solomon "was more lucky than wise," write Dixit and Nalebuff. "[H]is strategy worked only because of the second woman's error." The economists' interpretation, we should note, relies on a literality that many biblical scholars are careful to avoid in pursuit of less utilitarian insights.

138 **DAVID LEE ROTH:** See Jane Rocca, "What I Know About Women," *Brisbane Times,* April 7, 2013; David Lee Roth, "Brown M&Ms," online video clip on Van Halen's Vimeo channel, 2012; Scott R. Benarde, *Stars of David: Rock 'n' Roll's Jewish Stories* (Brandeis University Press, 2003); David Lee Roth, *Crazy from the Heat* (Hyperion, 1997); Mikal Gilmore, "The Endless Party," *Rolling Stone,* September 4, 1980. Portions of the Van Halen rider are posted on The SmokingGun.com; special thanks to Mike Peden for verifying the Van Halen rider details, via the files of Jack Belle.

144 **MEDIEVAL ORDEALS:** See Peter T. Leeson, "Ordeals," *Journal of Law and Economics* 55 (August 2012). For further Leeson reading, see "Gypsy Law," *Public Choice* 155 (June 2013); *The Invisible Hook: The Hidden Economics of Pirates* (Princeton Univ. Press, 2009); "An-*arrgh*-chy: The Law and Economics of Pirate Organization," *Journal of Political Economy* 115, no. 6 (2007); and "Trading with Bandits," *Journal of Law and Economics* 50 (May 2007). We are grateful to Leeson for his helpful comments on our manuscript.

149 **THE HIGH COST OF EMPLOYEE TURNOVER:** See Mercer and the National Retail Federation, "U.S. Retail Compensation and Benefits Survey," October 2013; Jordan Melnick, "Hiring's New Frontier," QSRmagazine.com, September 2012; and Melnick, "More Than Minimum Wage," QSRmagazine .com, November 2011.

150 **A WORKER WITH A FOUR-YEAR DEGREE EARNS ABOUT 75 PERCENT MORE:** See "Education at a Glance 2013: OECD Indicators" (OECD, 2013).

150 **ZAPPOS AND "THE OFFER":** See Stephen J. Dubner, "The Upside of Quitting," September 30, 2011; Stacey Vanek-Smith conducted the interview with Tony Hsieh and other Zappos employees. Thanks to various Zappos employees for follow-up interviews. / 151 **It costs an average of roughly $4,000 to replace a single employee:** See Arindrajit Dube, Eric Freeman, and Michael Reich, "Employee Replacement Costs," U.C.-Berkeley working paper, 2010. / 151 **A single bad hire can cost . . . :** Drawn from a CareerBuilder survey by Harris Interactive.

152 **THE SECRET BULLET FACTORY AND THE WARM-BEER ALARM:** Based primarily on author visit to the site, with follow-up correspondence with Yehudit Ayalon. See also: Eli Sa'adi, *The Ayalon Institute: Kibbutzim Hill—Rehovot* (pamphlet, available on-site).

154 **WHY DO NIGERIAN SCAMMERS SAY THEY ARE FROM NIGERIA?** This section was drawn from author interviews with Cormac Herley and from Herley's fascinating paper "Why Do Nigerian Scammers Say They Are from Nigeria?," Workshop on Economics of Information Security, Berlin, June 2012. Thanks to Nathan Myhrvold for bringing Herley's paper to our attention. / 154 **Dear Sir/Madam, TOP SECRET:** This letter is a mashup of various scam e-mails, a catalog of

which can be found at 419eater.com, a community of scam baiters. Our letter draws heavily on one letter in a 419eater .com thread entitled "A Convent Schoolgirl Goes Missing in Africa." / 157 **Firm numbers are hard to come by:** For overall fraud amount, see Ross Anderson, et al., "Measuring the Cost of Cybercrime," paper presented at the Workshop on the Economics of Information Security, Berlin, Germany, June 26, 2012; and Internet Crime Complaint Center, "2012 Internet Crime Report," 2013. / 157 **One California victim lost $5 million:** See Onell R. Soto, "Fight to Get Money Back a Loss," *San Diego Union-Tribune*, August 14, 2004. / 158 **Roughly 95 percent of the burglar alarms . . . are false alarms:** See Stephen J. Dubner, "The Hidden Cost of False Alarms," Freakonomics Radio, April 5, 2012; Rana Sampson, *Problem-Oriented Guides for Police: False Burglar Alarms*, 2nd ed., 2011; and Erwin A. Blackstone, Andrew J. Buck, Simon Hakim, "Evaluation of Alternative Policies to Combat False Emergency Calls," *Evaluation and Program Planning* 28 (2005). / 158 **False positives in cancer screening:** National Cancer Institute, "Prostate, Lung, Colorectal, and Ovarian (PLCO) Cancer Screening Trial"; Virginia A. Moyer, on behalf of the U.S. Preventive Services Task Force, "Screening for Ovarian Cancer: U.S. Preventive Services Task Force Reaffirmation Recommendation Statement," *Annals of Internal Medicine* 157, no. 12 (December 18, 2012); Denise Grady, "Ovarian Cancer Screenings Are Not Effective, Panel Says," *New York Times,* September 10, 2012; J. M. Croswell, B. S. Kramer, A. R. Kreimer, et al., "Cumulative Incidence of False-Positive Results in Repeated, Multimodal Cancer Screening," *Annals of Family Medicine* 7 (2009). / 159 **Millions of PC's sent into never-ending reboot:** See Declan McCullagh, "Buggy McAfee Update Whacks Windows XP PCs," CNET, April 21, 2010; Gregg Keizer, "Flawed McAfee Update Paralyzes Corporate PCs," *Computerworld,* April 21, 2010; and "McAfee delivers a false-positive detection of the W32/wecorl.a virus when version 5958 of the DAT file is used," Microsoft online support. More information can be found in Cormac Herley's paper. / 161 **"There's a chatbot psychotherapist":** See http://nlp-addiction.com/eliza/.

161   WHY TERRORISTS *SHOULDN'T* BUY LIFE INSURANCE: See Steven D. Levitt, "Identifying Terrorists Using Banking Data," *The B.E. Journal of Economic Analysis & Policy* 12, no. 3 (November 2012); Levitt and Stephen J. Dubner, *Super-Freakonomics,* Chapter 2, "Why Should Suicide Bombers Buy Life Insurance?" (William Morrow, 2009); and Dubner, "Freakonomics: What Went Right?," Freakonomics. com, March 20, 2012. / 164 **"I'm not sure why we're telling the terrorists this secret":** See Sean O'Grady, "Super Freakonomics," *The Independent on Sunday,* October 18, 2009. / 165 **Encouraging the guilty to "ambush only themselves":** Proverbs 1:18, *New International Version.*

CHAPTER 8: HOW TO PERSUADE PEOPLE WHO DON'T WANT TO BE PERSUADED

167   FIRST, UNDERSTAND HOW HARD THIS WILL BE: Much of this section is drawn from the work of the Cultural Cognition Project and author interviews with Dan Kahan and Ellen Peters as presented in Stephen J. Dubner, "The Truth Is Out There . . . Isn't It?," Freakonomics Radio, November 30, 2011. The CCP's website is an excellent resource for their work. For the climate-change topic, see Kahan, Peters, Maggie Wittlin, Paul Slovic, Lisa Larrimore Ouellette, Donald Braman, and Gregory Mandel, "The Polarizing Impact of Science Literacy and Numeracy on Perceived Climate Change Risks, *Nature Climate Change* 2 (2012). (For an earlier version of that pa-

per, see Kahan et al., "The Tragedy of the Risk-Perception Commons: Culture Conflict, Rationality Conflict, and Climate Change," *Cultural Cognition Project working paper no. 89.* Further information on the numeracy and science-literacy questions can be found in these papers as well as in Joshua A. Weller et al., "Development and Testing of an Abbreviated Numeracy Scale: A Rasch Analysis Approach," *Journal of Behavioral Decision Making* 26 (2012). / 168 **The vast majority of climate scientists believe the world is getting hotter:** See, e.g., Chris D. Thomas et al., "Extinction Risk from Climate Change," *Nature* 427 (January 2004); Camille Parmesan and Gary Yohe, "A Globally Coherent Fingerprint of Climate Change Impacts Across Natural Systems," *Nature* 421 (January 2003); Gian-Reto Walther et al., "Ecological Responses to Recent Climate Change," *Nature* 416 (March 2002); and Peter M. Cox et al., "Acceleration of Global Warming Due to Carbon-Cycle Feedbacks in a Coupled Climate Model," *Nature* 408 (November 2000). / 168 **But the American public is far less concerned:** See John Cook et al., "Quantifying the Consensus on Anthropogenic Global Warming in the Scientific Literature," *Environmental Research Letters* 8, no. 2 (May 2013). / 168 **Pew polls and attitudes about scientists:** See Pew Research Center for the People & the Press, "Public Praises Science; Scientists Fault Public, Media" (2009, Pew Research Center). / 171 **Terrorists, for example, tend to be significantly better educated than their peers:** See Alan B. Krueger, *What Makes a Terrorist* (Princeton University Press, 2007); Claude Berrebi, "Evidence About the Link Between Education, Poverty and Terrorism Among Palestinians," Princeton University Industrial Relations Section working paper, 2003; and Krueger and Jita Maleckova, "Education, Poverty and Terrorism: Is There a Causal Connection?" *Journal of Economic Perspectives* 17, no. 4 (Fall 2003). / 172 **Trying to** keep a public men's room clean?: See Richard H. Thaler and Cass R. Sunstein, *Nudge* (Yale University Press, 2008). / 172 "... We are also blind to our blindness": See Daniel Kahneman, *Thinking, Fast and Slow* (2011, Farrar, Straus and Giroux). / 173 "It's easier to jump out of a plane": Kareem Abdul-Jabbar, "20 Things Boys Can Do to Become Men," Esquire.com, October 2013.

173   HOW MUCH DID THE ANTI-DRUG CAMPAIGN CUT DRUG USE?: See Robert Hornik, Lela Jacobsohn, Robert Orwin, Andrea Piesse, Graham Kalton, "Effects of the National Youth Anti-Drug Media Campaign on Youths," *American Journal of Public Health* 98, no. 12 (December 2008).

174   SELF-DRIVING CARS: Among the many people who informed our thinking on the driverless-car future, we are especially indebted to Raj Rajkumar and his colleagues at Carnegie Mellon, who let us ride in their driverless vehicle and answered every question. / 175 Google has already driven its fleet of autonomous cars: See Angela Greiling Keane, "Google's Self-Driving Cars Get Boost from U.S. Agency," Bloomberg.com, May 30, 2013; "The Self-Driving Car Logs More Miles on New Wheels," Google official blog, August 7, 2012. (Our text contains updated mile figures from a Google spokesperson as of October 2013.) / 174 Ninety percent of traffic deaths due to driver error: Per Bob Joop Goos, chairman of the International Organization for Road Accident Prevention; also per National Highway Traffic Safety Administration (NHTSA) statistics. / 174 Worldwide traffic deaths: Most of the statistics in this section are drawn from World Health Organization and NHTSA reports. / 175 In many U.S. cities, 30 to 40 percent of the downtown surface area is devoted to parking: See Stephen J. Dubner, "Parking Is Hell," Freakonomics Radio, March

13, 2013; Donald Shoup, *The High Cost of Free Parking* (American Planning Association, 2011); Eran Ben-Joseph, *ReThinking a Lot: The Design and Culture of Parking* (Massachusetts Institute of Technology, 2012); Catherine Miller, *Carscape: A Parking Handbook* (Washington Street Press, 1988); John A. Jakle and Keith A. Sculle, *Lots of Parking: Land Use in a Car Culture* (University of Virginia, 2004). / 176 **Nearly 3 percent of the U.S. workforce . . . feed their families by driving:** From a May 2012 Bureau of Labor Statistics report. The largest single category is heavy trucks and tractor-trailers, with more than 1.5 million drivers. / 178 **In wealthy countries, this is easily the leading cause of death for kids:** Per the World Health Organization, the share of traffic deaths is lower in less-developed countries, where many children die from pneumonia, diarrhea, and the like. / 179 **During this period of zero airline deaths, more than 140,000 Americans died in traffic crashes:** See Stephen J. Dubner, "One Thought About the Two Deaths in Asiana Airlines Flight 214," Freakonomics. com, July 8, 2013. For the difference between car and plane travel as discussed in the footnote, we relied on statistics from the Federal Highway Administration (for car data) and the Bureau of Transportation Statistics (for airplane data).

180   HAVE WE MENTIONED THAT NAME-CALLING IS A REALLY BAD IDEA IF YOU WANT TO PERSUADE SOMEONE?: Among the most accomplished name-callers in the modern era is the *New York Times* opinion columnist Paul Krugman. A political liberal, he has referred to conservatives as "mean-spirited class warriors" who are "wrong about everything," who "quite literally have no idea what they're doing," and "have transitioned from being the stupid party to being the crazy party"—all in just three weeks' worth of columns. /

180 **Negative information "weighs more heavily on the brain":** See Tiffany A. Ito, Jeff T. Larsen, N. Kyle Smith, and John T. Cacioppi, "Negative Information Weighs More Heavily on the Brain: The Negativity Bias in Evaluative Categorizations," *Journal of Personality and Social Psychology* 75, no. 4 (1998). / 180 **"Bad is stronger than good":** See Roy F. Baumeister, Ellen Bratslavsky, Catrin Finkenauer, Kathleen D. Vohs, "Bad Is Stronger Than Good," *Review of General Psychology* 5, no. 4 (2001). For more on this subject from Vohs, see Stephen J. Dubner, "Legacy of a Jerk," Freakonomics Radio, July 19, 2012. / 180 **Negative events . . . make an outsize impression on our memories:** As the late, great historian Barbara Tuchman wrote in *A Distant Mirror: The Calamitous 14th Century* (Knopf, 1978): "Disaster is rarely as pervasive as it seems from recorded accounts. The fact of being on the record makes it appear continuous and ubiquitous whereas it is more likely to have been sporadic both in time and place. Besides, persistence of the normal is usually greater than the effect of the disturbance, as we know from our own times. After absorbing the news of today, one expects to face a world consisting entirely of strikes, crimes, power failures, broken water mains, stalled trains, school shutdowns, muggers, drug addicts, neo-Nazis, and rapists. The fact is that one can come home in the evening—on a lucky day—without having encountered more than one or two of these phenomena. This has led me to formulate Tuchman's Law, as follows: 'The fact of being reported multiplies the apparent extent of any deplorable development by five- to tenfold' (or any figure the reader would care to supply)." / 180 **Consider a recent study of German schoolteachers:** See Thomas Unterbrink et al., "Parameters Influencing Health Variables in a Sample of 949 German Teachers," *International Archives of Occupational and Environmental Health,* May 2008.

182   **IF BEING FAT IS A BAD THING, THEN EATING FAT MUST ALSO BE BAD:** See, among many others, Robert H. Lustig, *Fat Chance: Beating the Odds Against Sugar, Processed Food, Obesity, and Disease* (Hudson Street Press, 2012); and the research of Dr. Peter Attia of the Nutrition Science Initiative as discussed in Stephen J. Dubner, "100 Ways to Fight Obesity," Freakonomics Radio, March 27, 2013.

184   **THE ENCYCLOPEDIA OF ETHICAL FAILURE:** Author interviews with Steve Epstein and Jeff Green, as featured in Stephen J. Dubner, "Government Employees Gone Wild," Freakonomics Radio, July 18, 2013. See *Encyclopedia of Ethical Failure*, Dept. of Defense, Office of General Counsel, Standards of Conduct Office (July 2012); *Encyclopedia of Ethical Failure: 2013 Updates*, same publisher; and Jonathan Karp, "At the Pentagon, an 'Encyclopedia of Ethical Failure,'" *Wall Street Journal,* May 14, 2007.

185   **THE TEN COMMANDMENTS:** This version of the Ten Commandments is drawn from the Jewish Publication Society's 1917 English Translation of the Tanakh, with an assist from the version contained in Joseph Telushkin, *Jewish Literacy* (William Morrow, 1991). Throughout history and among different religious groups, the Ten Commandments have been rendered in a variety of ways due to differences in translation, interpretation, length, and the fact that they appear twice in the Torah, first in Exodus and then in Deuteronomy. It is also important to note that the first of the commandments isn't actually a commandment but rather a declaration. Accordingly, the list is known in Hebrew as *Aseret ha-Dibrot*, the Ten Statements, rather than *Aseret ha-Mitzvot*, the Ten Commandments. / 186 **Ten Commandments vs. the Big Mac vs. *The Brady Bunch*:** Drawn from a report by Kelton Research, "Motive Marketing: Ten Commandments Survey" (September 2007); and Reuters Wire,

"Americans Know Big Macs Better Than Ten Commandments," Reuters.com, October 12, 2007.

187 **CONSIDER ONE MORE STORY FROM THE BIBLE:** This can be found in II Samuel: 12. We are indebted to Jonathan Rosen for bringing to our attention how perfectly this story illustrated our point. Some of the words used to tell it here are his, as we could not improve upon them.

188 **ANTON CHEKHOV AND WHERE TO "CUT INTO" A STORY:** For this insight, we are indebted to a long-ago writing seminar taught by the great Richard Locke.

CHAPTER 9: THE UPSIDE OF QUITTING

190 **CHURCHILL AND "NEVER GIVE IN":** Transcript provided by the Churchill Centre at www.winstonchurchill.org.

190 **"A QUITTER NEVER WINS, AND A WINNER NEVER QUITS":** In 1937, a self-help pundit named Napoleon Hill included that phrase in his very popular book *Think and Grow Rich*. Hill was inspired in part by the rags-to-riches industrialist Andrew Carnegie. These days the phrase is often attributed to Vince Lombardi, the legendarily tough football coach. For another discussion of the idea presented in this chapter, with stories of several different quitters, see Stephen J. Dubner, "The Upside of Quitting," Freakonomics Radio, September 30, 2011.

191 **THE CONCORDE FALLACY:** See Richard Dawkins and H. Jane Brockmann, "Do Digger Wasps Commit the Concorde Fallacy?," *Animal Behavior* 28, 3 (1980); Dawkins and T. R. Carlisle, "Parental Investment, Mate Desertion and a Fallacy," *Nature* 262, no. 131 (July 8, 1976).

191 **OPPORTUNITY COST IS HARDER:** For a lovely and insightful essay that touches on the concept of opportunity cost, see Frédéric Bastiat, "What Is Seen and What Is Not Seen," *Se-*

lected Essays on Political Economy, first published 1848; published 1995 by The Foundation for Economic Education, Inc.

192 **MICHAEL BLOOMBERG AND FAILURE:** See James Bennet, "The Bloomberg Way," *The Atlantic,* November 2012.

193 **INTELLECTUAL VENTURES AND THE SELF-STERILIZING SURFACE:** Based on author interviews with Geoff Deane and other Intellectual Ventures scientists. See also Katie Miller, "Q&A: Five Good Questions," Intellectual Ventures Lab blog, August 9, 2012; Nathan Myhrvold, TEDMED 2010; and Nick Vu, "Self-Sterilizing Surfaces," Intellectual Ventures Lab blog, November 18, 2010. The primary patents on the UV self-sterilizing surface are numbers 8,029,727, 8,029,740, 8,114,346, and 8,343,434.

197 **THE *CHALLENGER* EXPLOSION:** See Allan J. McDonald and James R. Hansen, *Truth, Lies, and O-Rings: Inside the Space Shuttle Challenger Disaster* (University Press of Florida, 2009); also see Joe Atkinson, "Engineer Who Opposed Challenger Launch Offers Personal Look at Tragedy," *Researcher News (NASA),* October 5, 2012; and "Report of the Presidential Commission on the Space Shuttle Challenger Accident," June 6, 1986.

199 **THE "PREMORTEM":** See Gary Klein, "Performing a Project Premortem," *Harvard Business Review,* September 2007; Beth Veinott, Klein, and Sterling Wiggins, "Evaluating the Effectiveness of the PreMortem Technique on Plan Confidence," Proceedings of the 7th International ISCRAM Conference (May, 2010); Deborah J. Mitchell, J. Edward Russo, Nancy Pennington, "Back to the Future: Temporal Perspective in the Explanation of Events," *Journal of Behavioral Decision Making* 2, no. 1 (1989). Thanks to Danny Kahneman for bringing the idea to our attention.

199   **CARSTEN WROSCH AND THE TOLL OF NOT QUITTING:** See Carsten Wrosch, Gregory E. Miller, Michael F. Scheier, Stephanie Brun de Pontet, "Giving Up on Unattainable Goals: Benefits for Health?," *Personality and Social Psychology Bulletin* 33, no. 2 (February 2007). For a fuller treatment, see Stephen J. Dubner, "The Upside of Quitting," Freakonomics Radio, June 30, 2011.

200   **FREAKONOMICS EXPERIMENTS:** The website Freakonomics Experiments.com is still active as of this writing and can flip a coin for you, but the long-term tracking study is no longer functional. For Steve Levitt's fuller discussion on the topic, see Stephen J. Dubner, "Would You Let a Coin Toss Decide Your Future?" Freakonomics Radio, January 31, 2013. Perhaps the most heartbreaking write-in question we received: "Should I leave my son with my wife until she dies from cancer (approx. 8 months) so I can work in Africa to support my family, or should I turn down the job in Africa and stay in the U.S. to be near my son as I go broke?"

207   *COPS* **AND THE WRITERS' STRIKE:** See Associated Press, "Strike May Test Reality TV's Staying Power," November 27, 2007.

210   **WINSTON CHURCHILL AS "THE GREATEST OF ALL BRITAIN'S WAR LEADERS":** See John Keegan, "Winston Churchill," *Time*, June 24, 2001. Thanks to Jonathan Rosen for conversations on this topic and to the author and Churchill scholar Barry Singer for his continuing guidance on the topic.

If you have a question we haven't answered in these notes, or have something to share, feel free to drop us a line at ThinkLikeAFreak@ Freakonomics.com.

Index

Q&A with the Authors

When Think Like a Freak *was published in the spring of 2014,*
we embarked on a book tour that brought us to many cities in
the U.S. and the U.K. At some events, we'd be left to our own
devices, and we often wound up rambling on and on. At others,
we'd be joined by a professional interlocutor, who'd keep the
conversation on track. That was the case on May 20, when
Kishore Hari joined us onstage at the Castro Theatre in San
Francisco for an event sponsored by INFORUM, the Com-
monwealth Club's Innovation Lab. (You can find out more
about INFORUM at inforumsf.org.) Hari is director of the
Bay Area Science Festival at the University of California-San
Francisco; on Twitter, he's known as @sciencequiche, and de-
scribes himself as a "herder of nerds." We very much enjoyed
the spirited conversation with Hari and members of the audi-
ence—and hope that you will too, in this condensed transcript
of the event.

HARI: Gentlemen, welcome to San Francisco. So, I am one of those Freakonomics junkies and I have tried and failed miserably to apply the lessons from the book to my life, first of all with my baby's name, I tried to give him a name that was going to lead to global success.

DUBNER: If you want a name that leads to global success, Stephen—or Steven—seems to work pretty well. So what did you name the kid?

HARI: I named him Ira, because he is a three-year-old with the soul of an eighty-year-old Jewish man.

LEVITT: Let me stop you for a second, because I've had a hundred people come up to me and say, that was so cool, how you showed that the name you give to your child matters to their life, and half the time I say, no, actually we show the opposite, and the other half of the time I say, thank you, I'm really glad you enjoyed that. They're happier when I just say thank you, so more and more now, I just say that, but actually we did show it absolutely did not matter what name you gave to your child.

HARI: Take us into your relationship. How does it actually work between you two, because you don't live in the same city? So, how do all these amazing ideas get translated when you're so far apart?

DUBNER: So, I would say that every story on every page of the three books comes from one of maybe ten different ways. Sometimes, Levitt has done research and written an academic paper, and I then ask him to help me figure out the story to write, and we usually interview some other people to supplement it. Every story comes from just being observant, knowing people smarter than us, or at least smarter than me.

HARI: So what was the genesis of this book [Think Like a Freak]?

DUBNER: Our first book was much more successful than either of us could have imagined. We're very grateful for that, and we thought we should pack it in then. But we really enjoyed working together, so, four or five years later, we did a second book. We liked that one, and we thought maybe we should pack it in. We definitely didn't want to do a third book that was much like the first two. People write to us all the time, and we do read all the email, and we try to answer what we can, but we noticed that most of the questions were from people wanting to know how to fix stuff, whether it's something within their family, their community, their own job, politics or whatnot. We thought that rather than trying and probably failing to answer the questions, we would write a book that would deputize the world to think like this, because it's really not so hard.

HARI: Do you really feel like this is something that can be trained? It's so simple that anyone can learn how to—

LEVITT: We thought really hard about our approach, and I think we even surprised ourselves. To be honest, I thought our approach was much deeper than it was. I thought that we had come up with this brilliant inside tip no one has ever said before. Instead, we realized how much common sense goes into what we do. To start, in order to really have a chance, you have to be willing to say "I don't know." I've spent a lot of time in the last ten years around people in business and other settings who absolutely and categorically pretend to know the truth when they have no idea what they're talking about. And you simply get locked in if you can't say "I don't know." It's totally obvious, but most people don't think of it. So I think there's some value in being reminded of it.

HARI: Is that part of economics training, to say "I don't know?" It doesn't seem to jibe with what I see on TV. Paul Krugman is not on there saying, shrugging the shoulders, "I don't know."

LEVITT: That is true. It is absolutely a part of science and academics, and economists aren't scientists, but they are academics. An academic project might take you a year, and who's going to start on a project and spend a year if they know the answer already? But now in the era of people like Paul Krugman, who get up on TV talking, who always act as if they know the answers— I think people forget that those guys don't know the answers. I mean, the macroeconomy, no one understands the macroeconomy. It's a big, complicated mess, but you can't get on TV if you don't pretend you know the answers. When we get interviewed on those TV shows, the hosts are always surprised that we're willing to say we don't know. Kids are not used to this, because every public figure, every politician, now insists on looking confident, and looking confident means always knowing the answer or somehow answering a different question from the one he was asked so no one knows he didn't know the answer.

HARI: But you can face a lot of criticism for saying they "don't know." What effect does that criticism have on the work?

DUBNER: So literally within days of putting out a Freakonomics Radio podcast about saying "I don't know," and having the book released, we got all these good and inspiring examples of places that do it well or try to teach people to do it well. The military is one where people are basically given a handful of answers you can use if they are put on the spot, including "Yes, Sir," "No, Sir," and "I'll find out, Sir." According to everybody in the military I've talked to—and my brother was an Air Force pilot long ago—the premium is on knowledge and information, and maybe it's because they're in an institution where they're already getting beat up all the time. And unlike the rest of us, whose reputations are kind of inflated based on what we seem to know, a military reputation is based on what you actually know and can do, because there is a big difference between me sitting in a room typing words and my brother flying a plane. You really need to know. I love the idea that we're in a period where some institutions are building a culture where it is more encouraged to admit what you don't know. That said, it's still very hard to do, and the incentives conspire against it.

HARI: Let's talk about incentives, which is a big portion of your work. Why do incentives work, and why are they so important for us to take advantage of in the right ways?

LEVITT: We define incentives broadly, not just as financial incentives but also what we call social incentives, which is the approval and warmth of friends and colleagues, and then also morality, the moral incentives—what's internalized of the guilt you feel, which can also be a very powerful force. In defining incentives that broadly, it's almost redundant to say that incentives are really important, but every economist starts thinking about every problem by thinking about the incentives of various actors that are involved and it's important to include not just financial incentives but social and moral incentives. Social incentives are often the strongest. Peer pressure is overwhelming on humans as we know from fifty years of psychological studies that people will say and do anything if there's enough peer pressure. For an economist, where else could you start? How else would you ever start thinking about a problem? Although we know from politics that many people don't start there, that many people really start from a very moral place, asking what is right and wrong, or what does their religion say?

HARI: Did you say right off the bat, put away your "moral compass"?

LEVITT: Not everyone agrees with this, but our view is that it makes sense to put aside morality at the beginning. If you're interested in the answer to a problem, it is better to just understand the cause or relationship, to understand the deed and not to worry about where the data will take you, to simply understand the answers. A perfect example would be legalized abortion and crime. I had a theory that unwanted children are at risk for crime and other hardships. Legalized abortion in the United States led to fewer unwanted children, and so legalized abortion led to less crime. That has nothing to do with morality. It's just a statement of what we thought might be fact based on the data.

Then we looked to the data, and we found it to be true. Almost everyone else in the world thought about abortion in a moral perspective—either it's murder or it's a woman's right—which can confuse you and make it hard to actually think about what's going on. This is a great example where putting aside the morality allows you to start to understand the world. We know crime went down, did it happen because of this? We think so, the data seemed to support it. Now that doesn't say anything about what the right thing is, so then you have to bring the morality back in, which is okay. As we wrote in *Freakonomics*, no single person should change their stance on abortion because of what we found between abortion and crime, but that doesn't make it an unimportant result. For instance, a lot of people were saying we should be locking up more people in prison because crime had gone down because of prisons, but actually knowing that maybe it was due to legalized abortion helps inform choices, even if they are not the choices you would expect.

HARI: And so, how do you respond to those people who don't believe your conclusions?

DUBNER: I would argue that the proof in our chapter is compelling and convincing to many people. But our point is not to win every argument or to make every point. I don't really care so much if people agree or even like the stories. To me the point of telling the story is to convey a set of facts and circumstances in a truthful way that gives a sense of magnitude, that gives a sense of time, that includes statistics in a way that anybody can read it or listen to it and be a little bit more down the road toward thinking about things well. Because I'm a firm believer in the humanistic tradition that the more people who think about things well theoretically, the better the outcome is for everybody. If someone doesn't buy our argument on something, I think that's totally beside the point.

HARI: Do you not care as well if they don't agree with the conclusion that you're reaching?

LEVITT: I kind of live in my own world. I don't care very much about what other people think of me in general, so—

HARI: How do you have that superpower or you don't care about what people think about you?

DUBNER: I think that is a superpower.

LEVITT: I wasn't trying to be insensitive. I mean, I think, partly it was where I was raised. I was raised in a very unusual family. My mom was a psychic—

HARI: Your mom was a psychic?

LEVITT: Yeah, so my mom is a book channeler, if you know what that means—

DUBNER: A book channeler? Who has ever heard of a book channeler?

LEVITT: A book channeler is someone who goes into a trance and a higher being goes through her fingers and writes the book.

That was my mom, and my dad was the world's medical expert on intestinal gas—so I was kind of caught in the middle of these two worlds.

HARI: And economics was in the middle. I want to track back to thinking like a freak. What I took away was that we need to ask the right questions. Rather than asking what the solutions are, we need to figure out what are the right questions.

DUBNER: When you talk about problems like income inequality, poverty generally, famine, we tend to focus on the parts of the problem that disturb us, the very visible parts which are often not even the problem so much as the symptom. And then ideology gets involved, and there are a lot of arguments by people on every side, kind of shouting at each other, not really trying to persuade each other but just making their argument to prove how right they are. None of which is very productive. But you're right about asking a different question. Take income inequality. That's assumed as a terrible thing if it gets out of hand; what should be done about it? Is that the right question? I don't know, it's really hard. In the book, we tell a story of this hot-dog eating champion named Takeru Kobayashi who wanted to become the hot-dog eating champion even though he was this obscure, unknown, lightweight, college kid in Japan. We describe at great length the process he went through, and he arrived at a set of solutions that were entirely different than everybody else, because he essentially asked a different question.

HARI: What are some questions you are asking right now in research that are sort of a little bit unusual, that are sort of freakish questions?

LEVITT: I would say my favorite question right now—and it came out of the podcast—was the one we did on quitting, about why we think people just don't quit enough, and we had some theories about that.

HARI: This runs contrary to my entire upbringing basically—

DUBNER: We've all been brought up in a culture that says quitting is somewhere between moral and venal sin. It just doesn't make any sense. If you examine it even a little bit from the opportunity-cost perspective, it doesn't make any sense. I've quit a lot of things in life, and enjoyed it and benefited from it. Anyway, we did this podcast about quitting, and then Levitt turned it into an experiment.

LEVITT: Yeah, hundreds of people wrote us and said they were so inspired by the podcast they quit their job, divorced their wife, dropped out of school. After the podcast, we started a website, and we told people who had a problem to come to our website, and we'll help them make up their mind. We tried to help them think differently about their problem so that maybe they could figure it out. But if at the end they told us they still weren't sure, we said we'd really solve their problem. We said, heads, you leave your wife, tails, you stay with her. And forty thousand people came to our website to do it and, amazingly, of the people who came up heads, sixty percent of them followed the advice and did what heads was. When it came up tails, sixty percent did what tails said. So twenty percent of those forty thousand actually took an action based on our coin toss.

HARI: And you came up with big life decisions, I mean, this is divorce, but—but did they also come up with more esoteric decisions?

LEVITT: Yes, some were whether to get a tattoo or go on a diet. The data speak more clearly on this. If you're not sure if you should go on a diet, the data says you should go on a diet. The happiest people three or six months later are the people who go on a diet.

DUBNER: And seventy percent of the emails we received after the podcast were from people telling us they quit running. So plainly, everybody who's still running, give it up, because you know—

LEVITT: The way I would categorize the result is that it's pretty clear that the people who quit are no worse off on most things than people who don't quit. And it actually looks in many cases like they're happier. It's a funny thing, which I hadn't thought of before. The reason it is so hard to quit is that every day you face a choice: should I quit today or should I stick with it for one more day and quit tomorrow? Usually the quitting comes with pain—you have to tell your boss you're quitting, you have to tell your wife you're leaving or whatever, and it's very painful. So you always say, "I'd really like to quit but I'm just going to wait one more day." And the next day, you're in the same quandary.

The coin toss is interesting because many people told us that the coin toss actually gave a finality. The coin was in the air, which meant they had to decide what to do, and that freed them to actually know what they should do.

HARI: Did either of you guys use it?

DUBNER: I tried it to make sure it worked.

HARI: You tried to make sure the flipper flipped?

DUBNER: And I did quit running actually.

HARI: We're going to take some audience questions now. The first one wants to know what we worry about that we shouldn't worry about.

DUBNER: Almost everything. I hate to say it. But I am constantly astonished by how many people are convinced that the world is getting so much worse on so many dimensions, and then if you look at the actual dimensions they are talking about, the world is getting better on those dimensions. Life expectancy, crime, and a lot of these—in New York City, we're at record lows for deaths by fire, for instance. Just take something like that as an example. Years ago, that used to be a major problem. It's not the gains in human life and so on, it's how rapidly we assimilate those gains and then quickly move on and expect more.

LEVITT: One of the things for sure we should worry a lot less about is terrorism. Taking off our shoes in the airport and stuff like that. It's a lot of nonsense. But something I think we should worry about more—but I might be wrong—is pandemic. We have a great faith in the health system and the knowledge of doctors in medicines. But when it comes to things like really bad flus, like the 1918 flu, if one of those came, it would just ravage the world in a way that people can't even comprehend. I think the entire health system would shut down in a way.

HARI: How much of this is a hunch or do you have actual data to see?

LEVITT: So it's an informed hunch based on fact. One of the things we learned is that ERs recirculate air so if something really bad, such as spores or whatever, were to be floating around the air, the ER will need to be evacuated.

DUBNER: And hospitals, you know, there's no ROI on a zero-circulation room. So if you tell a hospital board they should build new zero-air circulation rooms because it will help in the rare event of a pandemic, no one wants to do that.

HARI: Another question. The book says intelligent people are often the most biased, with the most extreme views that they won't change. Should our government be made up of people who are less intelligent?

DUBNER: No. You want intelligence, but the challenge is teaching intelligent people to be less biased and that's really hard. So this research that we wrote about in *Think Like a Freak* is by a really interesting group called the Cultural Cognition Project.

It basically shows that the more education a person has, the more likely they are to hold an extreme view—on one end or the other—of a topic like climate change, nuclear power, and so on, which is puzzling. You would think that informed, educated people become the moderates, but it turns out that really smart people tend to be smart enough to have a very strong view and make it even stronger by seeking out evidence that confirms their bias. It's a hard problem, but it's really addressable. If you listen to, you know, the Far Left radio station every day, then listen to the opposite for a couple days a week. If everybody you know thinks a certain way, reads a certain set of books, has a certain set of ideas, it's possible you're all a hundred percent right all the time, but it's not very likely—and so to cross-pollinate is at least a hedge against having a bias so strong it would obliterate your ability to see another angle.

HARI: The next question is about data. They want to know if data is subjective considering that you decide what data you choose to use. What ensures impartiality?

LEVITT: That's a good question. The nice thing about data, most data, is that they're publicly available, and different people can look at the data and see if they come to different conclusions. I'm very much in favor of simple data analysis. At least I always start with just a portrayal of the data so that anyone can see the raw data that's in there. And then you can get into fancier things and put more of your personality into it.

HARI: Wait. Data has personality? You can put personality in data?

LEVITT: Absolutely. What the question said about data is of course true about everything, right? And probably less true of data than storytelling, a pure storytelling or anecdote or polling or whatever you would do. Yeah, I think many things you read are wrong, and we talk all the time about correlation versus causality. And what makes data so hard is that the only thing you actually see in the data directly is correlation, right? You just know whether two things tend to go together. Causality comes from something deeper. Causality is something which, absent a randomized experiment, you have to intuit or trick the data into revealing. And all we really care about is causality, and that's the fundamental challenge of social science in a world where you see correlations. How can you know causality? And that's where the art and the fun and the joy of what we do comes in.

HARI: Another reader wants to know if you have any thoughts on arguing with people and winning them to your side.

DUBNER: I used to teach this freshman-comp course at Columbia years ago. It was called Logic and Rhetoric. The approach isn't taught anymore, which is a shame because it's about making a good persuasive piece of writing, and you have to have a lot of logic and your rhetoric has to be good too. We have a chapter in the book called "How to Persuade People Who Don't Want to Be Persuaded," which is really, really hard. So we listed a series of rules of what you could try to do, and then some of the surefire things not to do. One of the surefire things not to do is insult people. A lot of smart people seem to forget this. Once you start personally insulting your opponent, there is no way he is going to come around to your side. Very few humans have a psyche strong enough (or weak enough) to do that. People who insult their opponent aren't really trying to persuade. They are trying to write their Op-Ed piece, to kind of preach to their choir and state their ideology, which is one thing, and fine, if that's what you want to do, but don't pretend you're trying to persuade.

HARI: You've been at this now for the better part of a decade. It's been eleven years since you first met. What are you actually hoping the legacy of *Freakonomics* is going to be?

DUBNER: That's a nice question. All right, I'll give a supernarrow and self-interested answer as the writer. I hope when my kids have kids, there are still books around, and I don't really care if mine are around, but I hope there are books around because I love the idea of that. I love doing this. I love doing a podcast, but to me, a book is a thing that has no equal. So anyway, my hope is that there are books and that maybe, you know, this will be one of them.

HARI: Do you have a hope for what the legacy will be after ten years?

LEVITT: No. I think we mostly just wanted to have fun and if other people have fun too that is great.

HARI: It's time for our last question, and it's an Inforum tradition to ask all of our speakers: What are your sixty-second ideas to change the world?

LEVITT: I mean, mine is really simple and really, really unpopular. I think that people should pay for their health care. And if you want to get really expensive treatments, you should have to pay a big chunk of that, and I think we should treat health and life and death more like a regular good. We spend nearly twenty percent of GDP on health care, and we need to—it's unfortunate, but we need to—make these horrible choices where we decide, are we going to send our kids to college or are we going to keep great-grandma alive for two more weeks, and the cost might be about the same for those two things. Right now, we shy away from those decisions, and we pretend like life has infinite value and that we can't make these choices. But either people will, or governments will, and I think that a really simple solution to health care is to give people catastrophic insurance, but to make them pay for what they use. The hospitals will stop charging, you know, seven thousand dollars for an MRI that has a marginal cost of seventy-five dollars, and I think the world would be a better place.

HARI: And Dubner, yours?

DUBNER: So I don't how to do this, but a project I've been working on as a writer for a long time, is to understand happiness better: what makes people happy and what makes people unhappy. For me, there are a lot of obvious triggers for what makes people unhappy, but once you drill deeper they are not as obvious. Poverty would seem to be an obvious one, but there are many people in poverty who are extremely happy. My family grew up in what would technically be called poverty. I was the youngest of eight kids with a copy editor for a dad who died when I was a kid, and we were this poor, rural farm family that if you look at us on paper, you'd say, "Oh my gosh, these poor people," and yet we were perfectly happy. I know many, many rich people who are miserable. What we think we know about happiness—what we actually know about happiness—could really fit on the head of a needle. And I think it's a shame that we've done so much as a civilization to produce so many wonderful things from food to technology, on and on and on, and yet we are in a state wherein we don't appreciate them very well. I am not saying we're wrong to not appreciate them, but I'm puzzled by it, and I would love to figure something out. Because I don't like so many people running around being so angry all the time. I think life is pretty amazing, and it would be better if everybody could lift everybody else up even just one percent. I would love that.

HARI: And, on that incredible uplifting note, let's give a big round of applause to the head freaks, Stephen Dubner and Steven Levitt.

About the Authors

Photograph by Vito Palmisano

STEVEN D. LEVITT, a professor of economics at the University of Chicago, was awarded the John Bates Clark medal, given to the most influential American economist under the age of forty. He is also the founder of TGG Group, which applies Freakonomics-style thinking to business and philanthropy.

Photograph by Audrey S. Bernstein

STEPHEN J. DUBNER is an award-winning author, journalist, and radio and TV personality. He quit his first career—as an almost-rock-star—to become a writer. He has worked for *The New York Times* and published three non-Freakonomics books. He lives with his family in New York City.

pp. 38-39   your Job (Tired)

SEX GOD

EXPLORING THE ENDLESS CONNECTIONS
BETWEEN SEXUALITY AND SPIRITUALITY